supersoul

a radical worldview for
a new consciousness

ian lawton

Rational Spirituality Press **RSP**

First published in 2013 by Rational Spirituality Press.
Second Edition 2014.
Third Edition 2016.
Fourth Edition 2020.

All enquiries to be directed to www.rspress.org.

A CIP catalogue record for this title is available from the British Library.

ISBN 978-0-9572573-3-7

Cover design by Ian Lawton.
Cover photograph by carloscastilla, licensed by dreamstime.com.
Author photograph by Simon Howson-Green.

supersoul, *sõóparsöl, n.*

A supersoul is a grouping of hundreds, maybe thousands, of souls. Myriads of supersouls are projecting individual soul aspects of themselves into this and myriad other realities, meaning they are very far from the ultimate consciousness. Yet to be fully connected to your supersoul is to have boundless wisdom and creative power, and as a full holographic representation of it you are already more divine than you can hope to conceive – divine enough, even, to nullify further speculation about what lies beyond.

CONTENTS

PREFACE

A significant portion of this book is based on evidence from out-of-body experiences. I am fully aware that most out-of-body explorers would tend to dismiss anything written by someone who hasn't had at least some relevant experiences of their own. Let me be clear that I haven't. I *have* tried, but I'm not a natural and I obviously haven't tried enough so far.

Yet this book is *deliberately* not based on any personal experiences of my own. What most interests me, indeed where my skill sets most lie, is in comparing the experiences and research of many others, then extracting the consistent elements and analysing them. To a significant extent this is what I did with the interlife experience in *The Big Book of the Soul*, and it's what I'm doing with the out-of-body experience here.

In fact I'd suggest that it's only by extracting these consistent elements from pioneers' reports that one can hope to reach any sort of objective conclusions and descriptions that are only minimally clouded by the more personal, subjective aspects of their experiences.

As always there are people who've assisted enormously with this work. Louise Caine helped me to overcome certain blocks that would otherwise have prevented me from even starting this journey. Christine Hanson lent me a whole stack of books at the outset. Katherine Membery provided great encouragement and feedback as I was drafting the early chapters. Jurgen Ziewe, William Buhlman, Frederick Aardema, Bruce Moen, Frank DeMarco and Tom Campbell all corresponded helpfully with me at various times.

Gordon Phinn not only supplied some of the finest research

1

material, much of it from his as yet unpublished *You Are History*, but also suggested other material and was always ready to act as a sounding board. He even took the trouble to read the finished manuscript and provide essential feedback, as did my personal friends David Chamberlain, Mike Forte, Lorna Franklin, Dave Haith, Neill Harris, Ken Huggins, Levon Litster and Lawrence Mills, most of whom are from our Spiritual Exchange meetup group in Bournemouth. Lorna and Levon in particular went way beyond the call of duty in bringing their considerable intellects to bear on it several times over – the former attempting to minimise my crimes against the English language, the latter to test my ideas to breaking point.

Last, but by no means least, the idea of *Supersoul* wouldn't even have seen the light of day were it not for the extensive conversations I had with my friend and colleague Todd Acamesis, as described in the opening chapter.

To all of you, thank you from the heart...

Ian Lawton
October 2013

The major change that has necessitated the production of a second edition so soon after the first is the development of a synthesised matrix model. I'm now firmly throwing my weight behind this, whereas before I'd been forced to leave my options open. Chapter 7 has therefore been heavily revised, with the inclusion of a lengthy section on the matrix model's implications, and a new 'set of principles' that arise therefrom. These now provide a firmer basis for the more radical and sophisticated supersoul model that emerges. Appendix I has also been added containing personal applications of the new model, but changes to other chapters are minor only.

I'd very much like to thank Gordon and Lorna again, and also Janet Treloar and Elena Adams, for letting me bounce the new model and its implications off them. This allowed me to gain some vital insight into how well it holds up to close scrutiny from people with different perspectives.

May 2014

While the third edition was mainly produced because of a new cover, with only minor changes to the contents, this fourth edition is quite the reverse. Chapters 1 to 4 and 8 have been substantially revised, but mainly for readability or to remove details that are no longer essential. In addition I've added some new channelled sources who support the basic concept of the supersoul into chapter 3.

By contrast chapters 5, 6 and 7 have been almost completely rewritten. The changes have mainly been motivated by feedback that some sections of the book were too complex, especially some of my attempts at mathematical modelling. I think to a degree this reflected my own confusion about the situation with regards to reincarnation when drafting the early editions. While I was questioning all aspects of this idea, I was really struggling to let go of it properly. This meant that even in the second edition I wasn't ready to ditch the various different 'models of soul consciousness' I'd put so much effort into developing. But I look back on them now and see just how much I was overcomplicating things – which just goes to show how thoroughly the concept of many lives was embedded in my consciousness. In any case now I've finally felt able to remove them completely, and hopefully this leaves a much simpler line of argument and evidence to show how I've arrived at the model of what I refer to as 'Supersoul Spirituality'.

December 2020

AUTHOR'S NOTE Comments in square brackets in quotes are mine, for clarification, while ellipses are used to indicate the omission of intervening words, sentences or paragraphs that are repetitive or irrelevant.

1

JOURNEY OF DISCOVERY

The *third* major shock to my spiritual system occurred on the evening of Friday September 7th, 2012. The scene was an Indian cafe in Wembley, north London, and sitting across from me was my friend and colleague, Todd Acamesis. An American by birth, he'd already established himself as a pioneering out-of-body (OOB) explorer in the UK.

He and I had met around eighteen months before at a party, and we hit it off straight away. For some time prior to that I'd felt there was very little that could alter my spiritual worldview. There might be occasional tinkering at the edges, but nothing that would force me to make *significant* changes – it was rare even for me to get excited by any spiritual books or talks. Yet when Todd started describing his OOB research that night I was spellbound. I had read Robert Monroe's pioneering *Journeys Out of the Body*, but here were new ideas that I'd never encountered before. I felt energised but also a little apprehensive. Some of them were so revolutionary I wasn't sure how well they meshed with the neat spiritual framework I'd spent years putting together, which wrapped me in its cosy cocoon just like a comfort blanket.

By one of those wonderful synchronicities we learn to appreciate deeply, when someone mentioned I was the 'famous author' Ian Lawton – something of an exaggeration but never mind – Todd strode out of the room and returned carrying his rucksack. "Well how d'ya like that?" he beamed, pulling out a copy of my

Wisdom of the Soul. "I was searching my shelf for a book to read on the train, and this just jumped out at me! I've had it for some time but never picked it up before." After what I'd already heard from him I was none too sure that my own use of the word *wisdom* was appropriate, but he politely waved away my concerns.

We agreed to meet in a pub in central London a few weeks later so we could talk some more. As he drew diagrams on scraps of paper about the different planes of our 'human hologram', and so on and so forth, I began to feel like a beginner again – not least because, instead of just *theorising* about them as I did, he had actually *visited* and experimented in them. Despite my anxiety about my newly discovered limitations, he even invited me to speak at one of his weekend OOB workshops. I agreed provided he let me attend the whole event.

It was a fascinating experience, but I didn't manage to achieve an OOB state then or during the month of regular practice that followed. I think it was through a combination of shame that I'd given up so easily, and of fear that much of what I thought I knew might need to be revisited, that Todd and I lost touch after this. I received occasional mailings from him, and sometimes replied to congratulate him on the way his 'Journey of Truth' meetup group in London was expanding and achieving wonderful things *on the ground*. He had hordes of people meditating and manifesting all over London, and they were clearly having huge fun into the bargain.

Indeed, because I'd been experiencing what I think it's fair to describe as an ever-worsening 'dark night of the soul' since we met.[1] So, although it was all I could manage not to be jealous, I finally wrote to Todd to get his views on our conflicting experiences, and he immediately replied that he'd get down to see me as soon as possible, which was extremely kind. As it turned out he struggled to make it to the wilds of North Dorset where I was living at the time, but he encouraged me to visit him in London. I was still apprehensive. I knew that we'd be bound to start talking spiritual frameworks again, and that there was a good possibility

I'd have to massively alter my own.

Around this time I visited my friend Louise Caine for some shamanic energy clearance and she convinced me I needed to pick up the baton again and face my fears. Thank heavens she had the foresight and intuition to push me in such an important direction.

My previous discussions with Todd had been pretty much brushed under the carpet in the intervening period, but now I dusted off the list of questions I'd prepared for him after our initial meetings. I tweaked them to allow for certain things I'd learned in the meantime, and then I was off to London. I rode up on the classic old 750 Honda I'd rebuilt in the winter, arriving at his flat with eyes on stalks from negotiating London traffic on a bike for the first time ever. Unabashed he immediately thrust me under his newly acquired 'lucid light' machine, despite my protestations that I was quite spaced out enough already. Nevertheless it was an interesting experience and we soon found ourselves relaxing in each other's company as if there had been no interlude.

It was no surprise to Todd that I had a long list of questions, and we started ploughing through them over dinner. The conversation was absorbing but intense, and now we'd arrived at probably the most crucial one of all – at least for me at this point. During our first meeting he'd explained that he'd recently met an incredibly wise entity called *Acamesis* in the highest planes he was able to access, and after several visits had been shocked to realise it was just another aspect of *himself*, or of his own oversoul as he called it. This was why he had recently changed his surname. But I'd had plenty of time to mull over this in the interim, and now I needed more: "Just how do you *know* he's part of you. How can you be so *sure*?"

His answer was swift and unequivocal: "Ian, you just *know*. In OOB exploration everything is about sensing different vibratory patterns, different frequencies of energy. The first few times I met Acamesis I was blown away, he felt like the highest, wisest form of intelligence I could ever meet... an angel or even a god in his own right. But then on one journey, when I'd calmed down a bit, it just

6

hit me that the vibrational pattern he was exuding had a special quality because it exactly matched my own. For all I know he was shielding me 'til I was ready for the truth."

Somehow I too just *knew* that was what he was going to say. In fact deep down I'd known he was right in his identification ever since he'd first mentioned the idea. I just hadn't wanted to accept that everything I thought I knew – that whole comforting, simple framework of spiritual understanding I'd spent more than a decade developing – was only scratching the surface.

But now it was all out in the open, fully in my conscious awareness. Now all fear fell away. Of course it didn't mean everything I'd written before was necessarily *wrong*, it had just represented a certain level of understanding. So now it was time to push on again into what was, for me at least, uncharted territory.

The *first* major shock to my spiritual system, the one that put me firmly on the path I've trodden ever since, came one fateful afternoon in the autumn of 1996 when I'd reached the ripe old age of 37. After a nominally Christian upbringing I'd rejected religion completely and plunged myself into the business world, first as a chartered accountant, then as a software salesman, and finally as an information systems consultant. I earned good money and spent all of it and more chasing the dream of following in my father's footsteps as a professional motorcycle racer – until the pain of too many broken bones and an obvious deficiency of talent forced me to switch to cars. Admittedly I think I had a growing sense of 'there must me more to life than this', but such intuitions tended to be ignored – until what was probably the most important synchronicity of my life forced me to pay attention.

I spotted a girl on the opposite side of my local high street and felt irresistibly drawn to follow her into a bar. That wasn't usual behaviour for me at all, but we got chatting and in no time she was telling me that we'd shared a past life together in Atlantis. This sounded like complete and utter nonsense but somehow I was fascinated, especially after I read James Redfield's seminal

Celestine Prophecy on her recommendation. The relationship we eventually began was pretty much a disaster, yet I owe Sarah everything for her perseverance in dragging me kicking and screaming onto the spiritual path.

It wasn't too long after this that the allure of the commercial world had faded so much I decided to get out. I just couldn't take its preoccupation with money, contracts, deals, deadlines, targets, progress, success and so on any more. I was self-employed by this time anyway, so it wasn't difficult to scale my activities right back. After a highly inconspicuous academic career when I studied Economics at UCL it was something of a surprise to find myself writing and researching alternative history, but that's what happened.

My first book, co-written with Chris Ogilvie-Herald, was an in-depth study of the famous pyramids called *Giza: The Truth*. It was published by Virgin in 1999, just in time to quell some of the more ridiculous internet-based rumours and speculation surrounding these monuments in the run-up to the millennium. It sold nearly twenty thousand copies worldwide and gained some degree of acclaim for being a grounded study not produced by academics with a supposedly vested interest. Apparently it served as a useful antidote to the sexed-up fictions being churned out by far better known alternative writers and I was, I hope justifiably, proud of the outcome of my many hundreds of hours of research. My new career had begun.

The *second* major shock came in February 2003. My editor had received the first draft manuscript of the follow-up, *Genesis Unveiled*. This was on the subject that had really fascinated me right from the outset – the idea of a forgotten, pre-flood civilisation of high culture and spirituality. But she was insisting that a whole new chapter needed to be inserted: "You talk about how there's evidence for the soul surviving and for reincarnation, and you use that as the backdrop for your theories about your forgotten race. But you never explain what the evidence you're referring to is!"

For some time I'd been familiar with some pioneering work on children who seemed to remember their past life, undertaken since the early 1960s by Professor Ian Stevenson of the University of Virginia. His scholarly, evidential approach to spirituality resonated with me hugely. But in broadening my search after the request from Virgin I stumbled across the equally pioneering regression research of his fellow countryman Michael Newton. Rather than just taking people back into their past lives, he had concentrated on their recall of the time *between* lives, or 'interlife' as I'd later call it.

I found his subjects' testimony incredibly compelling in its consistency, and all of a sudden everything in my developing spiritual worldview made sense. Most stunning was the idea that we're closely involved in *planning our own next life*, and the challenges it'll present us with so we can attempt to overcome them and grow. This too had an instant resonance. For the first time my eyes were opened to the fact that we really have to take personal responsibility for *everything* about our lives, and that there's no 'God's will' or 'judgment from on high'. We might receive help and advice from various guides and so on, but basically we each run our own show. This was a huge turning point for me.

After the second book came out I found myself concentrating solely on spiritual research, and extending my investigations to root out all the other interlife pioneers who had made similar discoveries, most of whom were far less well known. I also came to appreciate that whatever karmic dynamics shape our lives they have little to do with some supposed sense of right and wrong, and far more to do with gaining *experience* and seeing how we deal with different challenges from an emotional perspective. Best of all from my point of view, all this was based not on sacred texts from thousands of years ago, or on the diktats of some prophet or guru, but on the expanded-state testimony of hundreds if not thousands of ordinary people.

At the same time I was looking for more strongly evidential data to underpin what I was now calling '*Rational* Spirituality', from the areas of near-death experiences, of the aforementioned children who remember past lives, and of adult recall via past-life regression. The most compelling cases of the latter were provided by Peter Ramster, an Australian who brought three of his best subjects over to Europe to check out the accuracy of their memories. The results shown in his 1983 documentary were spectacular, because the facts they'd remembered in trance back in their homeland weren't only subsequently verified, but also *so obscure* as to be most logically explained by paranormal rather than normal mechanisms. In fact this is the key evidential 'acid test' that must always be applied in all these fields of research.

Thus the original *Book of the Soul* was born. Despite writing and researching in extremely difficult conditions it was completed in six months and in mid-2004, with Virgin completely shying away from such an overtly spiritual title and no offers from elsewhere, I published it myself. Over the next few years I went on to write a whole series of *Books of the Soul*, as well as developing the concept of the 'holographic soul', of which more later.

So why was Todd's experience of another, apparently far wiser, aspect of himself so crucial that it forced me to reappraise my whole spiritual framework?

The answer lies in the fact that by this point I could reasonably claim to be one of the foremost experts on the aforementioned interlife experience. I had exhaustively analysed all the pioneers' research; I had spent eighteen months attending Andy Tomlinson's 'Past Life Regression Academy' in order to qualify as a past-life and interlife regression therapist myself; and I had listened to recordings of a large number of his interlife sessions so that we could effectively co-author the two books *Exploring the Eternal Soul* and *The Wisdom of Soul*.

One key conclusion I'd already come to as a result of all of this was that the interlife experience was perhaps not quite as evidentially objective as I at first thought. Yes the pioneers had worked independently of each other and, until Newton came along, their books weren't widely read, making it no coincidence that the basic elements of the experience were consistently present in all of their work to varying degrees. What is more Newton performed a magnificent task in bringing the interlife generally, and the idea of responsibility for our own life planning in particular, to the awareness of literally tens of thousands of people – not least me because, as we've seen, he was entirely responsible for the second shock to my spiritual system. However he also produced something of a blueprint that was far more detailed than anything that had gone before, especially in his second book. Although he never released full case details or original transcripts of session recordings, I had come to realise – from working with my own clients, and from talking to fellow between-lives therapists – that he almost certainly must have been *leading* some if not most of his subjects to follow his blueprint far more than I'd previously appreciated. The same may be true of some, even many, of those who trained under him.

What I and my colleagues found was that the experience is far, far more fluid and varied than a reader of Newton's work would appreciate. Most subjects were reporting only one or two of the five main elements – unless they had already read up on the subject and been consciously influenced, which was increasingly becoming the case. What is more *some* who had read up on the topic nevertheless had an entirely 'non-standard' experience. So it was becoming increasingly clear to me that the contents of an interlife regression *can* be highly varied and almost limitless.

Most important for our current purposes, although many past-life regression subjects described reuniting with their 'higher self' or the 'core' soul energy they left behind when they came into incarnation, and although this was reported as involving an expansion of awareness to include other lives, it was hardly the same as meeting with the sort of independent, super-wise entity who was nevertheless another aspect of himself that Todd was describing. Nor did their descriptions of meeting with various guides and elders who assisted them with reviews ever describe these entities as being part of themselves. Where, then, did all this leave me?

Todd's answer as we sat in the café was simple. "From my experience, the planes you're referring to where interlife subjects review and plan are probably not the be-all-and-end-all that you've imagined them to be. They're still planes where there's a degree of illusion, one part of which is that souls residing in them still aren't aware of their greater oversoul and all its various aspects, or for that matter of the greater reality beyond them."

This was stunning to me. Yet again, I instinctively felt he was right. But our conversation was forcing me to recognise that the worldview I had written about, which was shared by at least tens of thousands of others, might be hopelessly inadequate. I had always assumed that souls journey through many lives in the earth plane in order to conquer all the emotional challenges it has to offer, before moving on to myriad other growth-oriented experiences, usually in other planes and environments. Yet here was apparent OOB evidence that there are somehow other aspects of *ourselves* who are already divine in their own right and have always had infinitely more power and wisdom – or, to be more precise, breadth and depth of consciousness – than I had ever attributed to even our reincarnating higher selves. Yet nor was Todd referring to the ultimate consciousness or 'Source', because he was quite clear there are many such oversouls. The straw that broke the camel's back was the idea that my beloved interlife experience might represent a relatively restricted view of the whole.

Over the next few weeks I read Monroe's second and third books, *Far Journeys* and *Ultimate Journey*, which I had bought after my first meeting with Todd but left on the shelf. As he had suggested they were completely different and far more revealing than the first, and they seemed to corroborate his experience.

I was both massively excited and disoriented all at the same time. I was desperately trying to make sense of this new way of looking at things. Quite what its full implications were I didn't know yet. But I *did* know that the idea that each of us is an integral part of a collective consciousness *so* wise, *so* powerful, even divine, yet at the same time still individualised – and 'personal' to us in a way that vague notions of some ultimate Source could never be – was becoming increasingly momentous to me. I also knew that this new worldview would be radical and revolutionary for huge swathes of spiritual seekers who like me had been weaned on a diet of traditional, regression-based, reincarnatory material – especially coming at a time of such wonderfully transformative potential for the human race as a whole.

Within three weeks of that fateful meeting in the Indian cafe I knew I had to write my first entirely new research-based book for more than five years. I woke up on the morning of the 27th September 2012 with the title *Supersoul* gifted into my consciousness. Everyone I discussed it with loved the whole concept.

I knew I was on the right track.

When I embarked on the research for this book I knew I'd be checking all the other OOB material I could lay my hands on, to see whether any of it would corroborate my emerging concept of the supersoul. This turned into more of a search for sometimes obscure material than I'd originally anticipated, and the results are revealed in chapter 4. But early on I also had a strong intuition that various channelled material might provide additional support, and that was my first port of call. Nor was I to be disappointed, as we'll find out in chapter 3.

I should point out that during this time it became clear to me just how much various OOB pioneers' reports of other realms dovetailed with the multitude of channelled reports of the afterlife from the last century or so. This research also led to the *fourth* major shock to my spiritual system, as we'll discover in chapter 5. In any case, as a result I resolved to write a state-of-the-art 'guide to the unseen realms' to bring everything right up to date, based on contemporary experiences and using modern language. Originally this was to have been incorporated into this book, but partway through I decided each topic was so huge that I could only do them justice by handling them separately. As a result volume three of this series – called, simply, *Afterlife* – was born.

In any case, while chapters 3 and 4 of this book lay out the evidential basis for the concept of the supersoul, before that we need to cover some background for comparison purposes, which we'll do in chapter 2. As for chapters 5 to 7, that's when things become even more interesting, because my research ultimately led me to places I'd never expected to go at all. In particular I found myself having to consider the true nature of time, and the idea that all lives – irrespective of the human era they appear to involve – are concurrent, that is being lived simultaneously in the 'eternal now'; the possibility that we live in a digital universe; and various concepts like parallel worlds and probable selves. These chapters don't make for easy reading because of the inherent complexity of the subject matter. Yet what comes out of them is a seriously radical worldview that challenges many 'sacred cows' of modern spirituality.

The final chapter wraps everything up by considering the full implications of the central contention in this book – which is that *each and every one of us* is an integral part of a collective of souls that has powers *way beyond* our normal imagination. The sort of powers we'd normally only associate with some sort of truly divine being. Although we should remind ourselves that there are myriads of supersouls operating just in our earth reality, and that they therefore represent a level of consciousness far removed from the ultimate Source – whatever that might be – this is still a mightily potent message for us to take on board at such a crucial time in human history. It may have been at least partially understood by certain esoteric and occult sects in previous epochs who devoted themselves to the understanding and expansion of consciousness, but if so it was heavily veiled and couched in terms

SUPERSOUL

that could never be digested by a mass audience.

Maybe this is the time to change all that.

Maybe *this* is the time when we, as the collective pioneers of a hugely exciting new stage in the evolution of human consciousness, are finally ready to put aside childish notions of an old man with a long white beard and flowing robes sitting atop a fluffy cloud making irrational decisions about our fate.

And to fully step into our own incredible power and birthright...

that of the SUPERSOUL.

2

CONCEPTS OF GOD AND SOURCE

...in which we'll compare the traditional *religions* of the Western and Eastern worlds, both with each other and with the sort of modern *spirituality* described in outline in the previous chapter. Overall we're interested in the attitude of each to a number of key questions: *Who or what is God? What is our relationship to him, her or it?* and *Do we have free will, and the power and responsibility to control our own destiny, or is it 'in God's hands'?*

The reason all this is crucial to our current enquiry is that the introduction of the concept of the supersoul has a direct bearing on, and indeed might persuade us to change our answers to, some or all of these questions. But we can't properly understand how and why without first laying out the attitudes of the various existing worldviews to these issues.

AN OMNIPOTENT GOD

At the end of the previous chapter I made what some might feel is a pretty harsh judgment of the 'childish' notion of God as 'an old man with a long white beard and flowing robes sitting atop a fluffy cloud'. I was of course satirising the sort of entirely anthropomorphic characterisation found in classical paintings, like Michelangelo's celebrated 'Creation of Adam', which depicts the two with arms outstretched and index fingers just making contact.

Admittedly this may have lost some of its relevance to contemporary followers of the three Abrahamic religions of Judaism, Christianity and Islam that predominate in the Western world. Nevertheless the key factor that unites all three is the extent to which they regard the ultimate power in the universe, for them Jehovah, God or Allah, as some sort of *external being*. Of course devotees of these religions vary enormously in the extent to which they follow this to its ultimate conclusion, and some would be rightly horrified by any suggestion that they don't take responsibility for the everyday practicalities of their lives. What is more I have nothing but admiration for those whose faith sustains them through life's challenges, often allowing them to be incredibly selfless in helping others or brave in standing up to oppression and tyranny. But it *is* an inescapable fact that a *strict traditional* interpretation of all these three religions is that followers can pray for help but, at the end of the day, their fate while incarnate is *not* in their own hands. Instead anything and everything that happens is 'God's will', and it doesn't help that he apparently 'works in highly mysterious ways'.

AN ALL-PERVASIVE SOURCE

If we now turn more to the East, Hinduism and its offshoots encompass a bewildering array of thought and belief, and this isn't the place to examine it all in detail. Suffice to say that some Hindus adopt a 'dualistic' philosophy, and conceive of the supreme god Brahman as an independent entity in a similar way to the Abrahamic religions. But the majority, especially those who ally themselves more closely to the original Vedic philosophy from which Hinduism sprang, see Brahman as a supreme energy that resides within every one of us. For them, the way to gain release from the addictive cycle of reincarnation is to see through the illusion of separateness from Brahman, thereby gaining release from the 'wheel of karma'.

This 'illusion model' forms something of a contrast to the

'experience model' that underlies the sort of typical, modern, reincarnation-based worldview to which I used to adhere and that I briefly referred to in the opening chapter. This regards the process of reincarnation as entirely natural and, indeed, exactly how experience is gained.

To delve a little deeper, for some the illusion model is interpreted as requiring that we should withdraw from earthly life and live in hermit-like seclusion. Yet this isn't what the great Hindu deity Krishna advised at all:[1]

> Not by refraining from action does man attain freedom from action. Not by mere renunciation does he attain supreme perfection. For not even for a moment can a man be without action. Helplessly are all driven to action by the forces of nature. He who withdraws himself from actions, but ponders on their pleasures in his heart, he is under a delusion and is a false follower of the path. But great is the man who, free from attachments, and with a mind ruling its powers in harmony, works on the path of karma yoga, the path of consecrated action. Action is greater than inaction: perform therefore thy task in life. Even the life of the body could not be if there were no action.

For others it requires that, while not withdrawing from the experiences of life, we should avoid strong emotional reactions to the circumstances we face – these being the generators of karma. This does seem to be the path recommended by Krishna:[2]

> The man who sees Brahman abides in Brahman: his reason is steady, gone is his delusion. When pleasure comes he is not shaken, and when pain comes he trembles not. He is not bound by things without, and within he finds inner gladness. His soul is one in Brahman and he attains everlasting joy. For the pleasures that come from the world bear in them sorrows to come. They come and they go, they are transient: not in them do the wise find joy. But he who on this earth, before his departure, can endure the storms of desire and wrath, this man is a Yogi, this man has joy.

This action-based but emotionally-balanced approach also tends to be associated with a relatively passive attitude of 'surrender', which may at least partly have something to do with the restrictions imposed by the Hindu caste system itself.

If we turn now to Buddhism, there are again many different strains. But to generalise massively its concept of rebirth follows similar lines to Hinduism in that the goal continues to be escape from the karmic cycle by banishing ignorance and seeing through the illusion. Yet it differs from more conventional notions of reincarnation owing to a different view of exactly what it is that returns:[3]

> Buddhism rejects the concepts of a permanent self or an unchanging, eternal soul, as it is called in Hinduism and Christianity. According to Buddhism there ultimately is no such thing as a self independent from the rest of the universe (the doctrine of *anatta*). Rebirth in subsequent existences must be understood as the continuation of a dynamic, ever-changing process of 'dependent arising' determined by the laws of cause and effect (karma) rather than that of one being, transmigrating or incarnating from one existence to the next.

It can be argued that Buddhism is far more a system of philosophy or a 'science of the mind' than a religion, but the drawback is that the many different strains have arisen due to philosophical wranglings over different interpretations of original Buddhist texts – and nowhere are these more prominent than in the interpretation of what *anatta* really means, and therefore exactly what is or isn't passed on in the rebirth process.[4] Suggestions include an 'evolving consciousness', a 'stream of consciousness', 'very subtle mind' or a 'set of mental processes'.[5] But whatever this is it clearly carries its karma with it, and consequently the somewhat simplistic notions of 'good and bad karma' influencing the quality and station of the new life – even whether it's as a human or animal and so on – remain pretty much intact from Hinduism.

This no-self approach has been taken to the extreme by that

contemporary strain of intellectual spiritual seekers who refer to themselves by the often misinterpreted term of 'Nondualists'. They tend to be characterised by an insistence that there's no such thing as the individual soul *at all* – let alone one that reincarnates – and that any appearance to the contrary is entirely illusory.[6] Yet this quite clearly flies in the face of the strongly evidential cases of the survival of individual consciousness separate from the physical body, as provided by both near-death and OOB research. This is backed up by the vast quantity of channelled material about continued existence and conditions in the afterlife, and of similar OOB material concerning experiences of the other planes, that has been amassed over several centuries and especially in recent decades. All this is presented in full detail in *Afterlife*.

But let's put aside concerns about possible misrepresentations of Nondualism, and about the apparent complexity and obscurity that surrounds Buddhism especially and Hinduism to a lesser extent. We can still thank their spokespeople – who include theosophists, of whom more later, various Eastern gurus who travelled West, high profile pop stars who travelled East, plus various psychedelic pioneers – for introducing the Western world to far more esoteric notions of God as an 'Absolute', 'Universal' or 'Ultimate' divine power that's *internal* to every one of us. As we've seen, to reflect its role as the original creative power that energises and permeates everything in the universe and to which everything eventually returns, this universal consciousness is most commonly referred to as 'Source'.

Of course the now hugely popular idea that everything is part of the 'One' or 'All', and that as a result nothing and no-one should be seen as *separate* from ourselves, is hugely powerful and important – not least because of the way it underpins the maxim 'what you do unto me, you do unto yourself also'. But there's an important rider to this. I would venture to suggest that we can have a sense of *individuality* without having to feel *separate*, because they're *not* the same thing.

SUPERSOUL

ONE YET MANY

If we *can* assume the existence of some sort of individual soul consciousness, or spirit, or whatever we want to call it, then is there any other way we can characterise its relationship with this universal, all-pervasive Source? Of course pondering this question isn't just the preserve of the formal religions, because throughout history spiritual philosophers, gurus and even channelled entities have sought to describe it. For example, in the mid-twentieth century the 'sleeping prophet' Edgar Cayce talked about aiming for 'more and more at-onement' with God yet remaining 'conscious of being oneself'.[7] Meanwhile Silver Birch, the entity channelled by Maurice Barbanell around the same time, asserted:[8] 'The Great Spirit has provided you with part of Himself... You are the Great Spirit and the Great Spirit is you.'

Yet two of my favourite sources of spiritual wisdom reveal that even the use of the word *part* to describe the relationship is misleading and inadequate. In the 'Pathwork Lectures' channelled by Eva Pierrakos for two decades from the late 1950s, the 'Guide' asserted:[9]

Every individual consciousness is universal consciousness. It would not be correct to state that it is a part of it, for a part implies it is only a little of it, a fragment of a whole. Wherever consciousness exists at all, it is all of original consciousness... [Nevertheless] individualisation is an integral aspect of the universal life power.

Similarly in the early twentieth century the Vedantic philosopher Sri Aurobindo, whose work we'll return to in chapter 4, made repeated attempts to define the intricacies of the relationship:[10]

The Universal exists but it does not absorb and abolish all individual differentiation... All is in each and each is in all and all is in God and God in all... The individual exists in the Transcendent, but all the Transcendent is there concealed in the individual... So it is with the One and the many, the finite

21

and the infinite, the transcendent and the cosmic, the individual and the universal; each is the other as well as itself and neither can be entirely known without the other and without exceeding their appearance of contrary oppositions... The infinite multiplicity of the One and the eternal unity of the many are the two realities or aspects of one reality.

All this brings to mind the Buddha's illustration of the concept of *anatta*, when he suggested that the flame of a new candle lit by a dying one is neither entirely the same nor entirely different. I would like to humbly suggest an extension to this. If we consider the flame from a powerful *furnace* used to light many small candles, we can more easily envisage this as a metaphor for a potential relationship between Source and the individual soul, rather than just between one life and another. Now if we appreciate that the flames are *both* the same *and* different, surely this idea has real and obvious potency? What is more it nicely illustrates that contemporary Nondualists are perhaps misguided in spreading a message of 'one *not* many', and that it should instead be amended to 'one *yet* many'.

THE HOLOGRAPHIC SOUL

Although in my early spiritual writings I held back because some people baulk at such supposed arrogance, in lectures and articles around that time I had less reticence about proudly declaring '*we are all God!*' For me the way in which this assertion gives us a real sense of our power over our own lives always had a huge resonance – indeed in the final chapter we'll discover the full extent of a creative power that's rarely conceived.

In any case a key breakthrough in this area was gifted to me in 2005. For some time I'd been aware of Michael Talbot's celebrated book *The Holographic Universe*, and I found the idea fascinating. But now it suddenly came to me that the modern principle of the hologram – a scientific concept that trailblazers like Aurobindo didn't have access to – should be applied to *soul consciousness* itself. This would really solve the apparent paradox and capture

SUPERSOUL

the nuances of the relationship between the individual and the universal. It would recognise the fundamental interconnectedness and unity of everything, while simultaneously accepting the validity of our individual experiences of the physical and other planes.

So the following year, while writing *The Wisdom of the Soul*, for the first time I formally laid out the simple yet I hope philosophically elegant concept of the 'holographic soul':[11]

Soul consciousness is holographic. We are both individual aspects of Source, and full holographic representations of it, all at the same time. However this does not mean that soul individuality is in itself an illusion. The principle of the hologram is that the part contains the whole, and yet is clearly distinguishable from it.

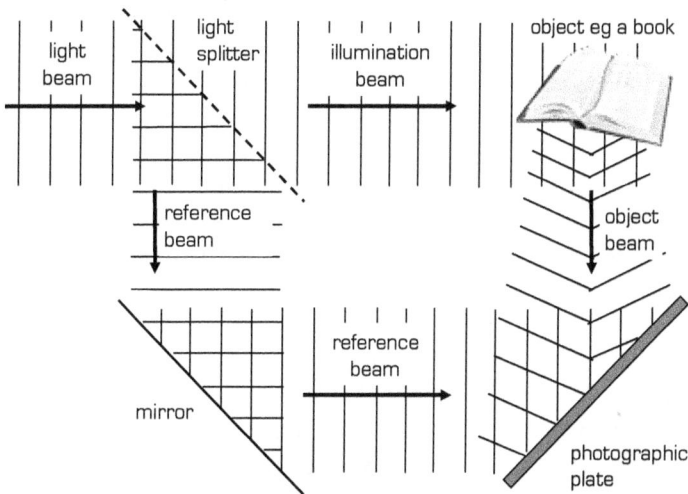

It is worth taking a little time out to understand the simple science behind this, using the accompanying diagram and words in italics that relate to objects shown therein. A basic hologram is created by shining a light beam through a *splitter* angled at forty-five degrees. Some of the light carries straight on through as an *illumination beam* that lights up all sides of an *object*, for example

23

a book. An *object beam* is then reflected off this at a forty-five-degree angle onto a *photographic plate* placed at a similar angle. At the same time the *light splitter* produces a *reference beam* that's bounced off a *mirror* angled at forty-five degrees and onto the *plate*, creating an interference pattern.

Whenever the plate is subsequently illuminated by the original reference beam, a holographic, three-dimensional image of the original object is created in its original position – even when the object itself is no longer actually there. But the crucial aspect for our purposes is that the photographic plate can be broken into increasingly small fragments, and *each one* will still reproduce the *entire* image – albeit with a slight loss of clarity at the extremes. This is what's meant by 'the part contains the whole and yet is clearly distinguishable from it'. In other words, again, we can have a sense of individuality without this having to imply separateness.

So far so good. But my original concept of the holographic soul clearly deals with the relationship between the individual soul and ultimate Source. So what happens if there are intermediate groupings of consciousness between these two? By the middle of 2011 I'd begun to follow the natural implications of my own theory, and to consider that there must be myriad holographic aggregations of consciousness from the micro level in the earth plane – for example, amongst clusters of cells that form organs – right the way through to various hierarchies and amalgamations of consciousness operating in other, increasingly higher, planes. The problem is I didn't have the sort of evidence that has since forced me to formally recognise what is clearly the most important of these groupings for our own earthly or human understanding – that of the supersoul.

We will consider how the theory of the holographic soul needs to be amended to cater for the existence of the supersoul in the final chapter. But for now, we can see just how powerfully the concept changes our view of who we really are – to the extent that my previous proclamation is now amended to '*we are the Gods!*'

WHY THE NEED FOR A NEW TERM?

Before we continue, let's be clear about the distinction between the term *supersoul* and various others with which it might be confused – indeed why I felt the need to coin a new term in the first place. First, in the last chapter we saw that the traditional reincarnatory concept of the 'higher self' is definitely not the same, because it's something that grows and expands with successive incarnations. By contrast the supersoul *starts out* with what we might call a divine level of awareness.

Next, some OOB pioneers use the word *oversoul* in the same context as what I mean by the supersoul. However this term tends to be more conventionally used in connection with universal consciousness or Source – most typically, for example, as a translation of the concept of *paramatma* in Hindu sacred texts.[12] It is also the sense in which the founder of the Theosophical Society, Madame Helena Blavatsky, used it in 1888 in her *Secret Doctrine*, when she referred to 'the fundamental identity of all souls with the universal oversoul'.[13] Remember my proposition is that, despite their divinity, there are *myriads* of supersouls operating just in our earth plane.

We also find in theosophical and other occult, esoteric and mystical literature the common idea of the 'group soul' or *egregore*. At its most obvious this can be thought of as applying to each animal species because, according to most sources, their soul consciousness isn't individualised in the same way as ours. But then for our species it can be applied at any collective level. For example, that of the whole of humanity, or of each major race or country, or of individual cities, towns, villages or even families – indeed of any group that shares a common interest or purpose. Again it's quite clear this is nothing like the concept of the supersoul.

The leading Qabalist Dion Fortune took a somewhat different approach in her *Cosmic Doctrine*, channelled in 1924 but not published until 1949. She used the word *oversoul* in connection with the 'logos' or overall consciousness of each solar system, which in her terms was the creator of that 'universe'.[14] She also referred to the 'life swarms' that filter down and back up through the various planes during each round of evolution, and to the fact that their aim is for their own group soul or oversoul to re-merge with that of the logos. But these groupings appear to encompass whole masses of entities and sometimes even humanity as a whole, so they too don't appear to represent the same concept as that of the supersoul.

Finally, nor should it be confused with the quite different notion of the 'soul group' encountered in interlife regression research and referred to in much spiritual literature. This refers to the groupings of individual souls with whom we supposedly share many lives, constantly changing our relationships to each other – from parent to child to lover to spouse to sibling to friend to enemy and so on. Yet there's no sense that these souls represent a genuinely collective consciousness to the extent that they're all effectively aspects of the same broader entity. What is more in the last chapter I questioned the validity of interlife material generally. Above all, channelled and OOB accounts of the afterlife planes singularly fail to bear out the concept of soul groups – as I discuss in more detail in *Afterlife*.[15]

So next let's go in search of the evidence for the existence of the supersoul, and start by sorting through various channelled clues left for us...

3

CHANNELLED CLUES

...in which we'll consider the issue of the reliability of channelled material generally, before turning to a variety of sources that appear to reveal the existence of the supersoul. Some are older, some fairly modern; some are well known, some hardly known at all; and while some only hint at the concept, several explicitly confirm it.

THE RELIABILITY OF CHANNELLED MATERIAL

Channelled material has almost certainly been with us for all time, although its popularity really took off in the Western world in the nineteenth century. In fact in recent years there's been an exponential surge of people wanting to learn to channel otherworldly sources – whether alone or in the company of a teacher – which in one sense is wonderful, but in another means that more than ever we need to appreciate such material is by no means infallible. The British occultist Dion Fortune was as coherent, honest and balanced as any channel and her various warnings on the matter are well worth restating:[1]

> Those who read these words may feel that I express first doubt, and then certainty: they are right; I express doubt of the accuracy of my own psychism, certainty of the reality of the Unseen. If I expressed certainty of my interpretation of my subconscious impressions, I should be claiming that which any

experienced and honest psychic knows that he cannot claim; if I expressed doubt of the reality of that which I am seeking to interpret, I should belie my sincerest beliefs, my deepest intuitions.

I came to occultism through the study of psychology, realising that there was so much more in the mind than the accepted theories accounted for, but at the same time realising that the psycho-analytic theories definitely accounted for a very great deal; I am obliged as a psychologist to recognise the part played by the subconscious mind in all mystic experience; I am obliged as a psychic to recognise the part played by the Unseen in much psychological experience.

Do not think that because a piece of information is obtained in an abnormal way it is bound to be true, any more than a thing is bound to be true because it is printed in a book... A spirit communication may come from a perfectly genuine spirit, and yet be valueless. Even if a man survives bodily death, dying is not going to cure him of being a fool; if he had no sense on the physical plane, he will not have any more on the astral.

If you set your front door open, the kind of person who would come walking in would be more likely to steal the umbrellas from the hall than undertake to instruct you in profound spiritual truths; and so it is with psychism: if you merely set the door of consciousness ajar you are more likely to get unpleasant experiences than spiritual teaching.

As for the process involved, Fortune and others have often described how complex information tends to be transmitted through symbolic and archetypal images.[2] But when these are translated by the channel they can only use mental constructs and vocabulary they already possess, so there's bound to be an element of approximation. That's even before we consider the extent to which someone is able to be a 'clear channel' by taking their conscious mind and knowledge off somewhere else so that it can't taint the information coming through.

As a psychologist Fortune also made the fascinating observation that her communications *might* have come from 'dissociated complexes of her own subconscious mind', although it's clear that wasn't her favoured interpretation, and nor was it that of her sources. But, who knows? As we'll shortly see it's a possibility that many angels and guides are no more or less than other aspects of our supersouls, so maybe the same is true of the wisest entities whose channelled messages have enlightened us down the ages – even if it was felt we weren't ready for this to be revealed until recently?

Whether or not this is generally correct, I found it was certainly the specific claim of several entities who began to impart their wisdom at around the same time as Fortune's sources. But before we consider them there are a couple of interesting forerunners.

THE REFORMER AND THE JOURNALIST

Our earliest channelled material of interest is a series of letters transmitted using 'automatic writing' by the American temperance reformer Julia Ames via the pioneering English journalist William Stead.[3] He had just started to discover his talent in this regard when Ames died young in 1891, shortly after he met with her for the first time, and her communications lasted for some six years – sometimes coming through daily, at others only after a lengthy gap. As with other spiritualists involved in public life he risked all his hard-earned journalistic reputation when he published them first in 1897, then republished them under the new title *After Death: Letters from Julia* in 1905. Her surname was deliberately not included, but in time her identity was established. As for Stead, he was one of the many unfortunates who perished in the Titanic disaster of 1912.

The letters are short and simple, but here is her most relevant observation:[4] 'We receive warnings [from our guides] as if they were the promptings of our own spirit. So they are... The guardian angel is indeed a kind of other self, a higher, purer, and more developed section of your own personality.' Of course guides and angels are typically thought to have the power to pull all sorts of strings behind the scenes, to get us out of difficult situations or whatever. So the idea that they're 'higher aspects' of our *own* selves or consciousnesses is a fascinating one that's hardly unconnected to the concept of the supersoul. Of course not everyone will resonate with it, but for me it reinforces the emphasis on personal responsibility and free will, and it means we're effectively *helping* ourselves – provided we're prepared to broaden our perspective of who we really are, and just how powerful we are.

Let us be clear that I'm not for a moment insisting there are no *independent* entities who help us in times of trouble and generally keep an eye on our wellbeing. There may well be some categories of angel, for example, that are entirely independent entities. What is more we'll find in the next chapter that many OOB pioneers are acting as guides themselves, helping to 'retrieve' souls trapped in other planes.[5] Even more fascinating is that to the recipients of this help they can appear divine and angelic, just because of the comparative radiance of their energy.

THE MYERS MESSAGES

Another early source of possible support for the concept of the supersoul again comes to us via automatic writing, this time that of the Irish medium Geraldine Cummins. Most notably she channelled messages from the late Frederic Myers, one of the founders of the Society for Psychical Research who passed on in 1901. These were published much later in two books, *The Road to Immortality* and *Beyond Human Personality*, published in 1932 and 1935 respectively.

The former contains a whole chapter dedicated to the idea of the 'group soul', which opens by describing it as 'one and yet many'.[6] This is a wonderful corroboration of the holographic nature of soul consciousness but, more important, unlike in occult literature Myers really *did* mean a group soul based not on earthly but on higher-plane connectivity. He suggested the group may contain 'twenty, a hundred, a thousand souls, the number varies'.

30

There is more to these messages, as we'll see in later chapters, but for now it's enough to propose that his concept of the group soul is surely closely connected to that of the supersoul.

Moreover, elsewhere he corroborates the ideas introduced in the last chapter – concerning the holographic nature of consciousness, and how retaining one's individuality doesn't have to imply separateness – when discussing the merger with the group soul, or even with 'the great source of spirit':7 'This... does not imply annihilation. You still exist as an individual. You are as a wave in the sea; and you have at last entered into reality.'

PHILIP IN THE SPHERES

Moving on several decades, our next potential source is a wonderful and little-known book from 1952 called *Philip in the Spheres*, based on the messages channelled by British medium Alice Gilbert from her recently deceased son. Unusually these involved the use of a strong telepathic connection already established during earthly life. But they also contain some brief communications from their joint 'unknown master', whose natural home was one of the higher planes and who occasionally came through to her instead:[8]

> True, I have no form which could manifest to you on earth. True, I am One with the whole, part of the measureless essence that *is*. Yet just as a chandelier has many points of crystal light and yet is One, so do we function. I feel, I think, I see and I love my children who work for truth, linked to me by the golden threads of thought...
>
> I am the unknown, to you, core of life, the person who is the light of your being and of those who work with you, including the beloved [Philip]... To me a flash of light which is you... speeds away and becomes detached as it plunges into the dark vortex of your earth. Yet there is for me a silver thread and along this flows your thoughts and your desire, your need and your emotion... On earth, it is for you to link with those who are also of my being.

This suggestion that the 'master' somehow encompasses the soul consciousnesses not only of Alice and Philip, but also of many others she needed to link with on the earth plane, is surely indicative of an aggregation of consciousness akin to the supersoul. What is more, just like Myers he makes clear that, although he's 'one with the whole', at the same time he retains his own identity.

SISTER FRANCES

Another channelled linkage that primarily relied on the use of telepathy was that of Helen Greaves and Frances Banks.[9] The latter was a strong personality who for many years led a rich and varied life as a Sister in an Anglican Community in South Africa, while at the same time acting as principal of a teacher training college and writing a number of books on education and psychology. She then returned to Britain where she and Greaves became firm friends, not least because of a shared love of Christian mysticism and deep meditation.

In 1965 Banks passed on from cancer aged 72 with Greaves by her bedside, and only three weeks afterwards they were able to re-establish their telepathic bond. Like some other non-professional mediums Greaves had initial concerns about ridicule if the messages she received were published, but her departed friend's forceful personality continued and she was persuaded of their importance. *Testimony of Light* was communicated over a two-year period although in two parts, with a seventeen-month gap in between.

A little like Myers she refers to the idea of 'soul groups' operating in the afterlife planes, but in her case these are made up of spirits engaged in particular fields of research – for example 'philosophers, scientists, researchers, priests, teachers' – who often then impress their ideas on various incarnate counterparts.[10] She continues that these groups are presided over by 'Great Beings watching over the progress of their cell-like cluster of souls' – which may be analogous to the concept of the supersoul, especially when we find that 'beyond these groups there must be other groups and companies of heaven, Greater Beings, vaster projects right up to the concept of Divinity Itself, of which we can have little or no conception'.

THE SETH MATERIAL

We now turn to the first of our sources that exclusively involves a 'higher-level' spirit, as opposed to one who has passed on to the other side relatively recently. The American medium Jane Roberts first made contact with the entity who called himself Seth in 1963, and together they produced what is commonly regarded as some of the finest channelled material ever gifted to humanity. Perhaps the most refreshing aspect – unlike predecessors such as Helena Blavatsky and Edgar Cayce, for example – is the clarity of his words and grammar, despite the complexity of the concepts he was sometimes attempting to put across. But just who was he?

Roberts herself pondered this question deeply. Like Fortune she was open to him being an independent entity or another part of her own psyche, although poignantly she favoured the interpretation that he was *both* at the same time. Here she describes her thoughts in the introduction to what many regard as his masterwork *Seth Speaks*, which was channelled verbatim in the first two years of the 1970s:[11]

> The whole creative venture may be the initiation of a personality, Seth, who writes books. Seth may be as much of a creation as his book is. If so, this is an excellent instance of multidimensional art, done at such a rich level of unconsciousness that the 'artist' is unaware of her own work and as much intrigued by it as anyone else...
>
> You can say that Seth is a dramatisation of the unconscious or an independent personality. Personally, I don't see why the statements have to be contradictory. Seth may be a dramatisation playing a very real role – explaining his greater reality in the only terms we can understand. This is my opinion at this time.

In the introduction to the subsequent *Nature of Personal Reality* Roberts was even more specific:[12] 'Seth's books may be the product of another dimensional aspect of my own consciousness not focused in this reality.'

Seth generally described *himself* as an 'energy personality essence no longer focused in physical form', indeed a teacher who had had many incarnations on earth. He referred to Roberts and her husband Robert Butts, who acted as the shorthand recorder of all the sessions, as Ruburt and Joseph respectively – these apparently being the names of their 'entire personalities' or 'whole selves'. As for his description of his relationship to them, I had to search long and hard to find the small handful of explicit confirmations of their connection, but this was well worth the effort. *Seth Speaks* contains a brief reference to it:[13] 'Initially Ruburt and Joseph and I were a part of the same entity, or overall identity.' Then I found that hidden in an appendix to the subsequent and lesser-known *Unknown Reality*, the two volumes of which expand on the ideas in *Seth Speaks*, was a similar reference originally channelled in 1964:[14]

> Ruburt and myself are offshoots of the same entity... And now, my dear patient Joseph, may I tell you that you are also part of that same entity – and this is one of the reasons why I am able to communicate with you both.

However one of the complexities in his material is the idea that we have multidimensional 'counterpart' personalities who exist in other 'probable realities', and we find here references to the Ruburt-Seth relationship couched in these more obscure terms too. The same applies to the entity 'Seth Two', who occasionally came through Jane instead of Seth, with a very different delivery. In this passage from *Seth Speaks* this clearly collective consciousness tries to give some idea of its nature and existence:[15]

> We are the voices who speak without tongues of our own. We are sources of that energy from which you come. We are creators, yet we have also been created. We seeded your

universe as you seed other realities. We do not exist in your historical terms, nor have we known physical existence. Our joy created the exaltation from which your world comes. Our existence is such that communication must be made by others to you... Because of the difficulties of communication, it is nearly impossible for us to explain our reality. Know only that we exist. We send immeasurable vitality to you, and support all of those structures of consciousness with which you are familiar. You are never alone. We have always sent emissaries to you who understand your needs. Though you do not know us, we cherish you.

Does this not this sound like a supremely divine consciousness – should we choose to use such a word – who helped to create this universe or reality, who encompasses the personalities of Ruburt, Joseph and Seth, and yet who clearly retains some sense of individuality and is *not* to be confused with Source consciousness? Elsewhere Seth backs this up by describing the huge power and potential of the 'multidimensional self':

You are the multidimensional self who has these existences, who creates and takes part in these cosmic passion plays, so to speak. It is only because you focus in this particular role now that you identify your entire being with it. You have set these rules for yourself for a reason... This multidimensional self of which I speak... has within it infinite sources of creativity, unlimited possibilities of development... It must find within itself ways to bring into existence those untold creations that are within it.

Meanwhile here he is talking about his greater consciousness, and about its holographic nature:

In larger terms, my soul includes my reincarnational personalities, Seth Two, and probable selves. I am as aware of my probable selves, incidentally, as I am of my reincarnational existences. Your concept of the soul is simply so limited... Each 'part' of the soul contains the whole – a concept that I'm sure will startle you.

He also describes how we tend to shut ourselves off from an awareness of our broader consciousness:

> As you become more aware of your own subjective reality you will therefore become more familiar with greater portions of your own soul. When you think of the soul as a closed system you perceive it as such, and close off from yourself the knowledge of its greater creativity and characteristics.

Again we'll return to various aspects of Seth's teachings in later chapters, but for now suffice to say they display such erudition and wisdom that to argue they come purely from Roberts' own *human* consciousness isn't just improbable but close to impossible. Unless, that is, she and her husband engaged in an elaborate hoax concerning the entire set of transmissions for more than two decades – something not even the most ardent sceptics tend to suggest. That being the case, Seth provides excellent corroboration of the concept of the supersoul. Not only that but if, as he claimed, both he and she were part of the same entity, we could have no finer proof of the wisdom available to us when we're able to connect up with other aspects of it.

GILDAS COMMUNICATES

The British medium Ruth White started receiving messages from her 'inner guide' Gildas in 1957, and for several years he merely advised her on personal affairs in conjunction with her psychologist Mary Swainson.[16] Then, in response to questions from the latter, Ruth began to channel more universal teachings by automatic writing. Within another few years a small group of interested parties had formed and the messages were disseminated to increasing numbers of people until, in 1971, the pair brought out *Gildas Communicates*.

One of his opening statements is highly pertinent to our current enquiry:[17]

> All souls belong to a group soul, and will eventually experience a unity with that group soul; when all parts are ready an

SUPERSOUL

ultimate group unity will be attained so that all that has been
seen as separate shall know itself to be whole and one.

But is he simply referring to some sort of ultimate reunion with
Source? Clearly not because he carries on: 'This is a stage of unity
which comes *long before* the final awareness of the complete
unity.' So he's quite clearly describing how we each belong to a
group of souls who are both separate and not separate – or, to put
it another way, each of us is a projection of a holographic
supersoul. Nor is that all, because he also corroborates my earlier
suggestions about guides: 'Usually, perhaps almost without
exception, the guides you are able to contact will be members of
your group – part of that group of entities which belong to the
group soul.'

FATHER ANDREW

The British medium Cynthia Sandys began to communicate with
her daughter Pat via automatic writing not long after the latter's
passing. In time so did Sally, the daughter of her friend and co-
author Rosamond Lehmann, then her husband Arthur and brother
Joe, until finally a whole variety of different spirits were
communicating through her. The first volume of her *Awakening
Letters* came out in 1978, the second in 1986.

One of her letters in the first was from Andrew Glazewski, a
Polish priest and polymath who helped to set up the excellent
Scientific and Medical Network – which is still going strong today.
In this he briefly describes meeting his 'greater self' in a context
that seems very much like that of his supersoul.[18]

THE MICHAEL TEACHINGS

Significantly better known than Gildas, although not as popular as
Seth, the original 'Michael teachings' were recorded in four books
by the American novelist Chelsea Quinn Yarbro between 1979 and
1995. They began to come through to the original channel Sarah
Chambers, to whom Yarbro gave the pseudonym Jessica, during an

impromptu after dinner session with a Ouija board in 1970.[19] Despite some initial scepticism and concerns, regular sessions of the 'Michael group' soon became the norm, with all members asking questions and transcribing the answers. Various people joined and left over the years but, by the time the twenty-fifth anniversary edition of *Messages from Michael* was produced in 2005, Yarbro was still a member and the group had been through five different channels.

Some controversy does continue to surround this group because it has always remained open to invitation only. Meanwhile Yarbro herself has denounced various 'imitators and frauds' who've apparently attempted to exploit the teachings by claiming to channel the same entity.[20]

I should also point out that a fundamental part of the teaching is to help people work out how far advanced they are in the conventional reincarnation cycle in terms of being infant/firstborn, baby, young, mature, old or infinite/transcendental souls.[21] I have always had something of an adverse reaction to anyone attempting to guess how far along they are on their spiritual journey – indeed, although I used to use words like *level* of spiritual *advancement*, I now avoid them like the plague because it encourages spiritual ego. What is more it's entirely misleading if the traditional concept of consecutive lives is fundamentally flawed because in fact they're all happening at the same time – an issue we'll return to in chapter 6.

That aside, early on the sitters asked for the name of whoever was communicating with them:[22] 'The last name a fragment of this entity used was Michael.' They then pressed for more information, and the response was highly revealing:

> Each soul is a part of a larger body, an entity. Each entity is made up of about one thousand souls... At the end of the cycles on the physical plane, the fragments once again reunite as we have reunited.

I am always somewhat sceptical of any attempt to attach hard and fast numbers and rules to spiritual ideas. Nevertheless again Michael's main thrust here seems to be highly suggestive of my concept of the supersoul. With reference to guides, Michael also reports that when we're in the earth plane we have access to help from other fragments of our 'greater entity' that are discarnate – although we only tend to use this when we're in trouble.[23]

CONVERSATIONS WITH GOD... OR SUPERSOUL?

We conclude this chapter with some fascinating passages in a recent and hugely popular body of channelled material. The three volumes of Neale Donald Walsch's *Conversations with God* were recorded by automatic writing and published between 1997 and 1999 – and in the first this is what his source has to say about *their* nature and identity:[24]

> Now I will tell you, there are even larger truths than this to which you will one day become privy. For even as you are the body of me, I am the body of another.
> *[NDW] You mean, you are not God?*
> Yes, I am God, as you now understand Him. I am Goddess as you now comprehend her. I am the conceiver and the creator of everything you now know and experience, and you are my children... even as I am the child of another.
> *[NDW] Are you trying to tell me that even God has a God?*
> I am telling you that your perception of ultimate reality is more limited than you thought, and that truth is more unlimited than you can imagine.

Then in the third volume his source gives a hint as to *our* true nature and identity:[25] 'What you call the individuated soul is huge, hovering over, in, and through hundreds of physical forms.' We will see much more of what they have to say about who we really are in later chapters, but for now these passages seem to point towards the concept of the supersoul.

So we've now reviewed a variety of channelled material from the last century that provides support for my concept of the supersoul more or less explicitly. But what's it like to actually *meet* one of these immensely wise, almost divine aspects of oneself? Let's find out...

4

OUT-OF-BODY ENCOUNTERS

...in which we'll introduce the phenomenon of OOB experiences (OOBEs), and discuss just why this is such an exciting area of consciousness research. Then we'll turn to the pioneers to see how much their work sheds important light on our search for the supersoul. As with the channelled material some are older, some fairly recent; some are well known, some hardly known at all; and while some only hint at the concept, several explicitly confirm it.

THE NATURE OF OOBEs[1]

The evidence suggests that all or at least the vast majority of us go OOB during sleep and this accounts for some, although by no means all, of our dreams.[2] Unfortunately most of us forget these most interesting aspects of our bodies' downtime as soon as we wake up, although occasionally we get flashbacks. But surveys and anecdotal evidence seem to suggest spontaneous, *waking* OOBEs, in which the subject remains fully conscious, are pretty common too.[3] Famous names reputed to have had such experiences include spiritual, religious and mystical figures such as Zoroaster, Ezekiel, St John, St Paul, Muhammad, various Catholic saints, Emanuel Swedenborg, Sri Yukteswar and Paramhansa Yogananda; and writers such as Goethe, DH Lawrence and Aldous Huxley.[4]

Just as with the typical near-death experience, many OOB subjects report an initial sense of hovering outside their earthly body, perhaps looking down on it with some confusion. They feel they're still in a body of sorts but usually report that it's lighter and more manoeuvrable. This may be about as far as the experience goes, or they may travel around to other rooms in their house or hospital and so on. Some will find themselves having incredible adventures flying high above the earth looking down at cities and oceans, while others will travel to different dimensions. In these they might meet with departed loved ones or guides, or travel through a vast array of environments that are sometimes very like earth and sometimes not, while more practised travellers may end up having incredible transcendental experiences in higher planes. It appears that just about anything and everything is possible. We should also be clear that there are 'lower realms' that can be scary and are best avoided. Of course because the planes they're visiting are exactly the ones we inhabit when our earthly life ends, their nature and the various types of possible experience are all described in great detail in *Afterlife*.

Classical techniques for inducing expanded states of consciousness include meditation, psychedelics, breathing exercises, mantras, chakra work, shamanic drumming, isolation tanks, even sleep and food deprivation, and some experiences in these states undoubtedly bear some relation to OOBEs. But a number of pioneers have pursued the ultimate goal of learning how to induce them *at will*, and in recent decades they've made huge strides in harnessing contemporary technology to assist the process – such as listening to carefully engineered soundtracks that stimulate certain areas of the brain, or the use of 'lucid light' machines.[5] Most of the pioneers' books mentioned in this chapter contain an abundance of practical advice about OOBE induction, while the art of 'lucid dreaming' – which has obvious parallels in that it involves establishing conscious control of a dream – is very much a first step on the road, and one that's becoming much better known and more widely practised.[6]

One key aspect of OOBEs that the pioneers had to learn the hard way is the thought-responsiveness of the other dimensions they visit. In the astral plane especially, the one closest to our earth plane in terms of vibration or frequency, merely to think or imagine something – be it a person, object, building, vista or whatever – is to instantly bring it into being. This can produce all sorts of confusing, even disturbing effects, especially for those who aren't used to using meditation to control their thoughts, or are holding on to strongly repressed or negative emotions. It also means that experiences in other planes tend to be somewhat subjective, requiring translation of images and sensations that are often completely novel to the beginner. Above all, in these planes we also tend to see what we *expect* to see, which is especially true of those with any form of strong religious conditioning. That is exactly why the best testimony comes from experienced pioneers who deliberately set the intention to explore these realms as objectively as possible, as many times as possible, comparing and analysing their results – and who've therefore learned, at least to some extent, to master the art of seeing through their many and beguiling illusions.

A huge number of OOB explorers have now shared their experiences in book form, going right back to the turn of the twentieth century.[7] Prior to the 1970s there weren't *so* many that I couldn't go through them all, thoroughly checking for evidence of the supersoul to support what I already had from Todd Acamesis and Robert Monroe. From that point on a plethora of books on astral travel and projection was unleashed to satisfy a growing demand, although from a reasonable sample I found that only a handful of these are relevant to our current enquiry. This is because either they tend to concentrate on techniques for inducing an OOBE, or their authors' travels were restricted to the near-earth plane – which for simplicity's sake we can characterise as the earth plane except as experienced by an OOB explorer, or by a departed spirit who remains trapped therein. But when in the mid-1990s the field opened up again to some excellent new talent who have been leading the whole field of consciousness research down exciting new avenues.

LEADBEATER AND BESANT

One of the earliest bodies of work relevant to our current enquiry is that of the theosophists, whose main movement was founded by Madame Blavatsky who we briefly encountered in chapter 2. Much of her writing was supposedly channelled by various 'masters' or 'mahatmas' who have incarnated across the world in all eras in order to help humanity move forwards, and several of whom she had apparently met while travelling in India and the Far East. But to provide a full context we should note that accusations persist that she wasn't averse to faking the mid-air materialisation of letters from them, especially during her early séances, while she has also been accused of plagiarising a variety of other works.

Even leaving all this aside, unfortunately her prose in the massive two-volume *Secret Doctrine* and its equally lengthy predecessor *Isis Unveiled* is so stilted as to be almost impossible to follow in places, which reduces the potential benefit of what was clearly a huge amount of committed and selfless work. But two of her successors within the movement, Annie Besant and Charles Leadbeater, wrote in a far more digestible style.[8] They were both prolific authors and speakers, and collaborated on a number of books in the early part of the twentieth century while based at the Society's Indian headquarters in Adyar. What is more they were both instrumental in fulfilling a prophecy concerning a new 'world teacher' when they discovered and nurtured a young Jiddu Krishnamurti – even though in time he would disown the Society and stand alone as one of the best-known teachers of Eastern wisdom in the Western world.

The aspect of their work that's rarely mentioned in OOB literature, which came as a surprise to me when I started researching Leadbeater for this book, is that what's normally referred to as his and Besant's 'clairvoyance' included *astral* clairvoyance. In our terms it seems they were engaged in nothing less than full OOB exploration of the other planes. Leadbeater talks about his experiences as early as 1899 in his book *Clairvoyance*:[9]

Another wonderful result which the full enjoyment of astral clairvoyance brings to a man is that he has no longer any break in consciousness. When he lies down at night he leaves his physical body to the rest which it requires, while he goes about his business in the far more comfortable astral vehicle. In the morning he returns to and re-enters his physical body, but without any loss of consciousness or memory between the two states, and thus he is able to live, as it were, a double life which yet is one, and to be usefully employed during the whole of it, instead of losing one-third of his existence in blank unconsciousness.

Why is this pioneering theosophical work not more widely appreciated in contemporary OOB literature? Perhaps it's because Leadbeater never gave precise details of the methods he used – he was restricted by a requirement for secrecy within the movement. The closest he got was asserting that such clairvoyance could only be reliably and safely developed by devoting oneself to the 'slow and toilsome path of self development', and thereby becoming noticed and taken as a pupil by of one of the Masters.[10] What is more, although he clearly didn't intend for this early book to be a manual for OOB techniques, his description of the key aspects of this path is a salient reminder to us all that advice to meditate regularly and use the 'power of now' isn't at all new:

> Let a man choose a certain time every day – a time when he can rely upon being quiet and undisturbed, though preferably in the daytime rather than at night – and set himself at that time to keep his mind for a few minutes entirely free from all earthly thoughts of any kind whatever and, when that is achieved, to direct the whole force of his being towards the highest spiritual ideal that he happens to know. He will find that to gain such perfect control of thought is enormously more difficult than he supposes, but when he attains it, it cannot but be in every way most beneficial to him, and as he grows more and more able to elevate and concentrate his thought, he may gradually find that new worlds are opening before his sight.
>
> As a preliminary training towards the satisfactory

achievement of such meditation, he will find it desirable to make a practice of concentration in the affairs of daily life – even in the smallest of them. If he writes a letter, let him think of nothing else but that letter until it is finished; if he reads a book, let him see to it that his thought is never allowed to wander from his author's meaning. He must learn to hold his mind in check, and to be master of that also, as well as of his lower passions; he must patiently labour to acquire absolute control of his thoughts, so that he will always know exactly what he is thinking about, and why – so that he can use his mind, and turn it or hold it still, as a practiced swordsman turns his weapon where he wilt.

More directly relevant to our current study, he also explicitly discusses travelling in the 'astral body':[11]

We enter here upon an entirely new variety of clairvoyance, in which the consciousness of the seer no longer remains in or closely connected with his physical body, but is definitely transferred to the scene which he is examining... The sight is much fuller and more perfect; the man hears as well as sees everything which passes before him, and can move about freely at will within the very wide limits of the astral plane. He can see and study at leisure all the other inhabitants of that plane... He has also the immense advantage of being able to take part, as it were, in the scenes which come before his eyes – of conversing at will with these various astral entities from whom so much information that is curious and interesting may be obtained.

He continues by discussing the even greater advantages of being able to use the 'mental body':

The vehicle employed is no longer the astral body, but a substitute manufactured for the occasion from the substance of the seer's mind-body – a vehicle, therefore, belonging to the mental plane, and having within it all the potentialities of the wonderful sense of that plane, so transcendent in its action yet so impossible to describe... The enormous advantages given by the possession of this power are the capacity of entering upon all the glory and the beauty of the higher land of bliss, and the possession, even when working on the astral plane, of the far more comprehensive mental sense which opens up to the student such marvellous vistas of knowledge.

Although the practice of projecting the consciousness has almost certainly been around since time immemorial, Leadbeater and Besant deserve great credit as being among the first to write about it in terms that most of us can understand. But, as if their mastery of the OOBE wasn't enough, they also provide by far the earliest potential support for the concept of the supersoul. Before we continue, however, it should be said that even interpreting their more easily digested material can be extremely difficult for those who don't devote themselves to theosophy wholeheartedly – which I don't – so what follows is just my best interpretation.

We must first appreciate that the highest divine conception they felt it useful to discuss was the 'logos', which as we saw at the end of chapter 2 is effectively the creator-god of each solar system. Although they clearly accepted that even more divine entities must exist beyond this, and that ultimately there was presumably something akin to what is so often referred to as Source consciousness, they didn't care to speculate too much on these. This was because to them even the logos itself was a consciousness we couldn't possibly hope to engage with while still incarnate in the earth plane. This is an eminently sensible approach with which I've come to agree wholeheartedly.

The theosophical conception that bears most comparison with the supersoul is that of the *monad*, which is conceived of as an emanation from the logos. This word normally denotes a 'prime, indivisible unit' of some sort, but unsurprisingly Blavatsky's use of it was varied and extremely hard to follow.[12] Meanwhile in her 1898 overview *The Ancient Wisdom* Besant refers to the 'monadic group souls' of the mineral, vegetable and animal kingdoms, which are clearly not comparable to supersoul.[13] But when she turns to the more evolved human monad, the context seems to change somewhat, with some holographic-soul style discussion of the interplay between the 'precious essence of individuality' of the human soul and the 'essential unity' of the monad. Importantly, given what we'll find out about the driving force that motivates all consciousness in a later chapter, it's also referred to as 'the receptacle of all results, the storehouse in which all experiences are garnered'.[14]

Even more useful for our current purposes, in *The Monad and Other Essays* that was published two decades later Leadbeater provides a somewhat clearer picture by describing it as 'our personal God, the God within us... a triple light of blinding glory, yet possessing certain qualities by which one monad is somehow distinct from another'.[15] Somewhat confusingly he also refers to our 'ego-soul', whose relation to the monad isn't entirely clear to me, but apparently even this is 'a glorious being' who, when encountered, might be thought of as 'some splendid angel'.[16] He expands on this wonderful confirmation of Acamesis's experience as described in the opening chapter by asserting that, as long as we're 'led on little by little', we become 'able to face without flinching glories which would dazzle us if they burst unexpectedly upon our view'.[17] He also describes experiencing a oneness with what I'd refer to as the other projections of his supersoul:

> At this level man still has a definite body, and yet his consciousness seems equally present in vast numbers of other bodies. The web of life... is extended so that it includes these other people, so that instead of many small separate webs we get one vast web which enfolds them all in one common life.

On that basis I'd tentatively suggest that theosophy *may* provide some of the earliest support for the concept.

AUROBINDO

We mentioned Sri Aurobindo briefly in chapter 2. He passed over in 1950, and eighteen years later his spiritual collaborator Mother Mirra founded the 'universal city' of Auroville in Pondicherry, Southeast India. His letters, compiled into *The Integral Yoga* in

1993, make it clear that he regarded the OOBE or 'exteriorisation' as an important tool for spiritual growth, provided it was used under correct supervision.[18]

However his master work is the lengthy, two-volume *Life Divine*, the majority of the contents of which stem from articles originally written for his monthly journal *Arya* from 1914 to 1919. The main thrust of this hugely erudite book is an attempt not only to realign Hindu Vedanta philosophy with its original Vedic roots, but also to integrate it with modern science and metaphysics. As a result in many crucial respects Aurobindo's arguments and conclusions form a stark contrast to those of most Eastern gurus and mystics.

This work is certainly not easy to follow, but for our current purposes two of the many concepts he discusses are *overmind* and *supermind*. Typically these are characterised as planes, the former representing the highest one that plays host to individualised consciousness, the latter consisting only of 'unity-consciousness'.[19] Yet elsewhere they come across, in very simplified terms, as two different representations of the fundamental unity of Source itself. We also find him making the following brief yet tantalising statement:[20] 'The overmind releases a million godheads into action, each empowered to create its own world.' Clearly even these godheads are extremely powerful, and it may be that either they or his concept of overmind may bear at least some relation to that of the supersoul.

YRAM AND LARSEN

The next OOB pioneer who contributes to our search is electrical engineer Marcel Forhan. Writing under the pseudonym 'Yram', his *Practical Astral Projection* was originally published in French in 1925 and reflected fourteen years of OOB experiences.[21] While most of his contemporaries such as Vincent Turvey, Oliver Fox and Sylvan Muldoon seem to have restricted themselves to the near-earth planes, he 'travelled from dimension to dimension, not satisfied until he had attained that almost indescribable state when one is no more than a unity-multiplicity with the higher energy of nature'. Again this is a wonderful prelude to the holographic nature of soul consciousness, but there is much more to Yram's work.

His was a wide-ranging and highly esoteric take on the OOBE, and his worldview was probably more Taoist than anything else. Meanwhile his ideas on the underlying mechanics of space-time, energy and consciousness were intellectually challenging and possibly ahead of their time and deserving of further study in the present era – although I don't have the expertise to form a proper judgment. Most importantly for our current purposes he devotes a whole chapter to describing the different characteristics of various 'Great Beings' he encounters in 'higher worlds', including Jesus.[22] He also provides a description of the presumably similar 'supermen-gods' he meets on his travels:[23]

> We learn of the existence of supermen, whom our ancestors used to consider as gods. The extraordinary power of their auras, the perfection of the qualities one recognises in them, the perfect mechanism of the dimension where they are to be found, surpass in simplicity all that men could have imagined concerning the gods.

Meanwhile this prescient prediction about OOB research is surely just coming to fruition now, nearly a century later:[24] 'I am not exaggerating in claiming that the propagation of this particular knowledge will cause humanity to enter into a new evolutionary period.' We will expand on this idea in the final chapter.

Another early pioneer who is equally enlightening, albeit with a far lighter touch to her writing, is Caroline Larsen. A Dane who moved to Vermont, she had her first spontaneous OOBE in 1910 when already in early middle age. By the time she published *My Travels in the Spirit World* in 1927 she'd had many, many more spanning the entire spectrum of the other planes, always accompanied and assisted by the same guide.

Most relevant for us is her account of travelling beyond our solar system and on into the 'abyss of space', where like Yram she was overwhelmed by entities of incredible radiance:[25]

> Spirits of high superiority and authority such as I had never
> seen even in the fourth plane passed in every direction, singly
> and in larger or smaller groups. A white light of intense power
> emanated from each, and enveloped them in a flaming
> radiance, that varied in intensity in proportion to their spiritual
> power. All were garbed in glowing white. The combined
> brilliancy of the light thus produced flooded all space. The great
> whirling globes were as nothing to this awe-inspiring spectacle.
> The mere sight of these majestic spirits even from afar was
> enough to convince the beholder that they were the rulers and
> controllers of the whole universe, of matter and of spirit. The
> overpowering dominance of their personalities subdued my
> spirit so that, staring and stupefied, I trembled and shrank at
> their presence.
>
> Two in particular, a man and a woman spirit, burned with
> the light of two flaming suns dimming all others near them with
> the intense lustre of their white radiance... Dazzled, I cowered,
> raising my hand to my forehead in an involuntary tribute of
> humility and awe... They appeared to be gods rather than
> perfect spirits, yet I was informed that they had once dwelt in
> human form... By spiritual development they had risen to the
> highest power, and, as my guide explained, they were now a
> part of that Supreme Power that rules and guides both the
> material and spirit universe... It was a glorious moment for me
> when I beheld these marvellous beings, and knew the
> happiness of their close presence.

Of course these descriptions of dazzling entities mirror those of
Acamesis and others.

OPHIEL, TWITCHELL AND ATTESHLIS

We now move forward more than three decades to the 1960s and,
whilst collations of other people's experiences from Robert
Crookall and Celia Green are probably better-known, there are
several lesser-known sources who at least provide important
background information for our study. The first is the occultist and

51

OOB pioneer Edward Peach. Writing under the pseudonym 'Ophiel' his *Art and Practice of Astral Projection*, published in 1961, is a detailed instruction manual that unfortunately contains no details of over thirty years of personal experiences. But he makes an important contribution in other ways. In particular his suggested reading list of Leadbeater, Besant, Dion Fortune, Israel Regardie and Aleister Crowley explicitly reinforces the linkages between OOB exploration, theosophy, Qabalah, Rosicrucianism and other occult and even magical approaches to transforming and expanding consciousness.[26]

What is more it appears this may only have been the tip of the iceberg. Most religions throughout the ages have in one way or another attempted to provide their adherents with the means to commune with God or other divine beings, and we've already mentioned meditation and various other approaches to achieving expanded states of awareness. But the extent to which this may often have involved the specific aim of taking consciousness OOB and focusing it within other planes seems to have been deliberately masked from popular awareness.

This was certainly the claim made by Paul Twitchell in 1969 in *Eckankar*, which is translated as 'the ancient science of soul travel'. As well as the more celebrated cases of supposed OOB travel by various Abrahamic religious figures mentioned at the beginning of this chapter, he suggests that this was the main modus operandi of the Egyptian and Greek mystery schools, and of classical Greek figures such as Pythagoras, Socrates and Apollonius; of Hindu mystics such as Kabir Das and Goswami Tulsidas; of the founder of Sikhism, Guru Nanak; of Sufi mystics such as Shamus Tabrizi, Jalaluddin Rumi and Hafiz; and of any Tibetan lama.[27] Other researchers have augmented this list with the ancient Chinese and Japanese, the Romans, and various indigenous tribal cultures around the globe.[28]

Twitchell himself supposedly spent twenty-five years training under an Eckankar or ECK master in Tibet so that he could bring its science to the Western world.[29] I should mention that his teachings incorporate the complete elimination of sexual and other 'destructive' passions; nonattachment to all persons or things; and an excessive delineation of the subdivisions within the other planes, and of their gods or rulers and even 'capital cities'.[30] But for our current purposes his most important contribution is to suggest that the deities that exist even on the lower planes have often been mistaken for 'God' by various less-experienced religious mystics while OOB, whilst mere 'friends and kin' in the mental plane are regularly mistaken for angels.[31]

As for the use of OOB exploration in esoteric Christianity in particular, some fascinating insights come from the work of the Cypriot mystic and healer Stylianos Atteshlis, who also went by the name of 'Daskalos' or 'teacher'. By the age of seven he was 'already able to self-consciously travel to the worlds of the higher dimensions' by the use of what he refers to as 'exosomatosis' – that is, the OOBE.[32] Then until his death in 1995 he devoted himself to teaching small groups, although latterly his messages reached an increasingly international audience.

The best summary of his thinking is *The Esoteric Teachings*, which first appeared in Greek in 1987 and was translated two years later. For our current purposes his description of how the 'One contains the multiplicity' clearly ties in with the concept of the holographic soul.[33] Even more to the point, his work takes a rather more theosophical turn when he refers to the ' Holy Monad' that can radiate many of its rays out into different realities:[34] 'It can choose to extend its own radiations, not only through the Human Idea, but also through other Archangelic Ideas and into other universes'. What is more he makes it clear that each Holy Monad isn't Source itself but just 'one of countless myriads of cells within the multiplicity of Absolute Beingness'. Does this sound like the supersoul?

MONROE AND THE INSPECS

Apart from Leadbeater, none of our OOB sources has so far identified *themselves* with the higher beings they describe –

although it could just be that humanity simply wasn't ready for such revelations in that era. In any case this all changes now we come to the man who really blazed the trail for all his successors, and who remains undoubtedly the most influential OOB researcher of modern times – Robert Monroe, who we met in the first chapter. A highly successful broadcaster who ended up with his own radio and TV network, he had his first spontaneous experience in 1958 while in his forties, and when it happened several more times he increasingly devoted himself to exploring the phenomenon. Although he could apparently be somewhat challenging to deal with, his books back up his reputation as a highly intelligent man with widespread interests who was fastidious in his approach to his research, and in particular to the documentation and analysis of his huge number of OOBEs. He had nearly six hundred in the twelve years leading up to the publication of his seminal *Journeys Out of the Body* in 1971.[35] And by the time he passed into the realms he knew so well in 1995 he'd made huge strides in advancing our knowledge of the phenomenon and, perhaps most importantly, given thousands of ordinary people the comfort that they weren't going crazy.

Yet we shouldn't gloss over the fact there are some problems with Monroe's trilogy. First, his love of acronyms will get on your nerves if you don't share it. Second, although some questions raised in one book are resolved in another, some of the most interesting ones – especially relating to our main theme – are left unanswered even by the end. Third, he uses so many different names for different aspects of his consciousness that it's virtually impossible to be sure what's what; whether some are the same or not; and whether, when some descriptions even appear to contradict each other, that's because he wasn't writing clearly, or was confused himself, or was deliberately holding some material back. Fourth, although his first book is by far the best known, the most interesting material tends to be found in the follow ups, which are somewhat overlooked.

In fact the only information of any relevance to the concept of the supersoul in the first is the enigmatic ending to a chapter about angels and helpers:[36] 'Someday, perhaps, the helpers will identify themselves. I suspect the answer may be surprising.' Despite its popularity Monroe was in no hurry to complete a follow-up, although it's interesting to note that he took a great interest in the Seth material and visited Jane Roberts at her home in 1973.[37] Then in 1985 after an interval of fourteen years *Far Journeys* hit the bookshelves, and we again encounter the helpers that he realised had been directing his OOB explorations all along, mostly unseen and silent. Their reward was to become the beneficiaries of one of his least endearing acronyms: the INSPECS, or 'intelligent species'. This is the sense of awe one of them inspired in him the first time he deliberately set the intention to meet one properly:[38]

> A bright light, very intense, glowed in front of me, first ovate, reshaping into a tall humanoid form, so bright I cringed from it. For what seemed an eternity I shrank back, trying to shield myself from the brightness. Then I began to cool down until I was no longer uncomfortable, and I could tolerate the brightness.
> *[INSPEC] Is that better for you?*
> 'Better' was an understatement. Much longer and I would have melted.

Of course the sense of divinity such entities inspired in Monroe and his predecessors closely resembles biblical reports of various prophets shrinking from the intense brightness of God's presence – a point not lost on him. In any case he gradually calmed down as the discussion progressed through a variety of topics, before returning to the true identity of the INSPEC:

> I was rapidly losing my sense of awe. It was replaced with a great feeling of warmth, of understanding, much of the order of old deep friendships, yet filled with intense respect, not the usual pattern of expected angels, if that is what they were.
> *[INSPEC] We can quickly grow wings if you wish.*
> No, no, please, no wings. No halos either, although... I could

understand how humans with limited but definite momentary superconscious vision could add a halo to make the human-formed INSPEC stand out as different. A brightly radiant form? How often in human history has such perception taken place?..
    [INSPEC] No doubt at all...
    Could that infer we as humans, the nonphysical energy part of us, actually are INSPECS and we don't know it?

Monroe was clearly getting closer, but the full truth only emerged some time later once the INSPECs had fully prepared him for entry into their realm proper. We will leave his main description of this experience of merging with other selves for the final chapter, but for now this is the revelation made by the now 'collective entity' at the end of the encounter:[39] 'We know who we are, and one I laughs and we all laugh at the name this I [Monroe] had given us. We are an INSPEC, just one. There are many others around us.'

So there we have it. A wonderful description of an immensely powerful group entity made up of many aspects or projections, including Monroe himself. As I explained in the opening chapter, this was the corroboration of Acamesis's accounts that convinced me I was on the right path.[40]

This fine pioneer's books aside, his legacy was actually secured just as much by his founding of the Monroe Institute in 1972. Here he and his small team of assistants embarked on a program that aimed to inject as much scientific, objective credibility into OOB research as possible. This included experimenting with 'binaural beats' to synchronise the two sides of the brain, allowing different brainwave states to be reliably maintained at different 'focus levels' – which turned into the 'Hemi-Sync' technology in widespread use today.

MCKNIGHT, MOEN AND BUHLMAN

One of the early participants in the Monroe Institute program was Rosalind McKnight, and her experiences over the next eleven years formed the basis of her first book, *Cosmic Journeys*, although it didn't come out until 1999. In this one of her invisible helpers enigmatically reveals that 'we are a dimension of a higher level of this being'.[41] Later their spokesman goes a little further:

> I am on the same consciousness level with this entity, we are one and the same, yet we are separate... I say that we are one and the same because groups of souls work together on certain levels or rates of vibration. Those souls working together on a given level could be considered 'group souls'...
>
> We work together as a group. I say a group, but it is a soul level. Every soul has its level and rate of vibration. As a result there are souls connecting on a direct rate of vibration – souls that have worked together closely throughout many ages of earth time and before the earth time, and who will work together beyond the earth time.
>
> A group soul is a part of every being and every soul. However, many souls are at a level in the earth existence where they are not aware of their oneness with other levels of consciousness.

If we now move on to McKnight's 2005 book *Soul Journeys*, these are based on OOB explorations guided by a being she refers to as 'radiant lady', who reappeared to her in 2003 after a forty year absence.[42] What's particularly fascinating for us about her youthful interpretation of this beautiful being who appeared by her bedside one night is that she had a 'strong sensation that she was a part of her'. What is more on her reappearance the guide herself reveals that 'their energy fields were connected in a very special way'.

Another attendee of multiple courses at the Monroe Institute was Bruce Moen, an engineering consultant, who then produced the four-volume *Exploring the Afterlife* series between 1997 and 2001. In the first, *Voyages into the Unknown*, he reports how one evening in 1991, while listening to Monroe describing one of his higher-level experiences, he was taken back to a spontaneous OOBE he'd had seventeen years beforehand during which he'd explored a vision of a 'disk' connected to a humanoid form via what looked like a kind of fibre optic cable.[43] Moen had never understood that vision until this point, but suddenly everything fell into place – he realised *he* was the humanoid form. This is how he summarises it:

> I discovered there is another me. That me is something I call my *Disk*... Others might call this the *Higher Self, Greater Self* or *Oversoul*. The me inhabiting my physical body is but one small part of the Disk. In my explorations, I've seen my Disk or Greater Self. To me, it looks like a large disk with many small, round lights arranged in concentric circles. It is my understanding each of these lights is a personality of my Greater Self... These 'other me's', if you will, maintain their personal identity as individual parts of my Greater Self. They didn't lose their personal identities when they became members of my Disk, rather, they added all within themselves to it. Each individual became an integral part of my Greater Self.

In book four, *Voyage to Curiosity's Father*, he returns to the theme of the disk vision and, in attempting to establish how many of them are involved with our 'earth life system', is shown 'perhaps ten or fifteen, but knew there were more'.[44] He also finds himself investigating *behind* his own disk, and sees a similar fibre optic cable emerging from it that connects to a larger parent disc – a pattern that's repeated until he reaches number eight. This clearly supports the idea I introduced towards the end of chapter 2 that consciousness operates at potentially infinite different levels of aggregation.

Let us now turn to probably the best-known successor to Monroe as an OOB explorer and teacher, William Buhlman, who runs regular workshops at the Institute. He has been journeying for decades and has written a number of books, in particular *Adventures Beyond the Body* and *Adventures in the Afterlife*, published in 1996 and 2001 respectively.[45] The former contains several fascinating descriptions of meeting and even merging with higher aspects of himself, to which we'll return in the final chapter.

Meanwhile the latter summarises an international survey of the experiences of some 18,000 participants from forty-two countries, and contains a number of their less discerning descriptions of meetings with 'beautiful, white angels' or 'an angel dressed in white sitting on a cloud', even 'a huge ball of light that I immediately knew was God'.[46] This clearly demonstrates the difference in quality of perception and interpretation between an experienced explorer of the higher realms and an occasional visitor.

Unsurprisingly given his transcendental experiences, when I contacted him while researching this book he corroborated the basic concept of the supersoul, although using some of the alternative terminology already discussed at the end of chapter 2:[47] 'The idea of the oversoul resonates with what I have experienced. I generally use the term *higher self* to describe this wise and powerful aspect of myself.'

BRUCE, TAYLOR AND PHINN

Australian Robert Bruce has been having OOBEs since he was four years old and his *Astral Dynamics*, first published in 1999 and heavily revamped ten years later, is regarded as a classic practical manual. However in terms of our current enquiry the only relevant material is his echoing of the view that our higher self is the invisible helper that always assists us when OOB.[48]

Albert Taylor is a former NASA engineer who began having consciously directed OOBEs in the early 1990s. In his 2000 book *Soul Traveller* he briefly discusses the concept of the oversoul as follows:[49]

> Last, but not least, is the oversoul entity, a being of unimaginable capabilities and possibilities. This type of self-aware consciousness is virtually unlimited... The oversoul entity has been referred to as a god in the making... The oversoul is rapidly progressing towards the ultimate truth, which is to become a coworker and cocreator with God. I believe this is the irrevocable destiny of the soul.

Unfortunately there are no reports of him meeting with such an entity, but surely it's reasonable to suggest he's referring to something very much akin to the supersoul. What is more we'll return to further similar descriptions of its – our – incredible creative power in the final chapter.

Moving up to Canada, Scottish-born OOB pioneer Gordon Phinn is a student of theosophy and an avid reader of all material related to other planes of consciousness, so his correspondence with me has been lively and extremely helpful. His first book, *Eternal Life and How to Enjoy It*, came out in 2004 and was an account of the afterlife that his guide 'Henry' had begun to channel six years earlier. His second, *More Adventures in Eternity*, came out four years later and moved more into lucid dreaming and OOBEs. The first part contains some wonderful channelled descriptions by various guides about their work retrieving trapped souls, while in the second he turns to his own extensive experiences of such activity in lucid dreams and, subsequently, via meditation using Hemi-Sync tapes – this inspired by reading Moen's books.[50] In this he corroborates the true nature of many guides and angels:[51]

> Such soul connections are usually translated into the acceptable frameworks of 'angel', 'deity', 'saviour', 'saint', 'demon', 'spirit guide' and 'prophet'. That the beings indicated by such terminologies really exist is not to be denied, but on many occasions that 'light of inspiration' is actually one's [own] soul.

In addition, although he's not explicit about his perceived relationship to his shape-shifting, anarchic and enigmatic guide Henry, he does say this second book was written by 'a committee of Gordons, two of whom are called Henry and Higher Self'.[52] Meanwhile he too uses the term higher self or monad to denote the supersoul, and during one of his 'conversations' therewith it revealingly explains why he's being given access to such high level information while still incarnate:[53]

> It is because you accept and understand my existence [and

influence] over and above many of my other personality projections through space and time; they either have no inkling of my existence, or they so identify me with either an angelic or godlike nature that they fall into the trap of praise and worship.

His third book, *You Are History* came out in 2015. It contains a further fascinating insight the perspective of his higher self:[54]

I do not recall 'coming into being', it would seem that I 'always was'. It is common amongst us, the cosmic clowns of the monadic plane, to say we are drops of divinity in an ocean of divinity, or sparks of light in a sea of light. En masse we make up the body of god. Perhaps we are not beyond counting, but I have yet to encounter one who really cares enough to undertake the task. We are parts of the whole just as you are. Together you make up humanity, together we make up god. And just as humanity does not actually speak with one voice, neither does god. When you as individuals speak with who you assume is god, you are actually talking with your Higher Self. It is as if a pet dog, in communing with its master, felt as if it were dialoguing with humanity, when actually it is dialoguing with a member of humanity...

There are of course, many belief systems extant in your world which insist that many beings and attributes are not of god at all, but are emanations of, or are perverted by, dark, demonic forces of one label or another. For us monads, repositories of the vast majority of human and sentient experience on earth throughout history as we are, this is just not so. We are hotels, as Gordon once put it, for good and bad guys alike. Victims, victors, the handsome, the ugly, the smart, the stupid, it's all the same to us as we head toward a totality of experience upon this unique planetary experiment.

ZIEWE AND AARDEMA

German explorer Jurgen Ziewe is a UK-based artist who's been having OOBEs for more than four decades. In his 2008 book *Multidimensional Man* he explicitly confirms that 'we are our own guardian angel, spirit guide and mentor'.[55] Moreover on his website he evocatively describes what he calls his 'silent companion', which he refers to elsewhere as his 'higher aspect or soul':[56]

> This light is like no physical light at all, more like a space lit up, a stillness which was wherever I was, a presence of luminosity right beside me. It felt as if it smiled the moment I turned my attention towards it after tearing myself away from the wondrous sights surrounding me. It regarded me like a child, lost in its world of play and like a loving parent accepting its child with love and joy the moment it turned away from its play, fully assured that it would not be left out of sight for a single moment, no matter how far it strayed. At any time I could enter into the light wholeheartedly and it would accept me with joy and without reservation.
>
> It was this reassurance which made me linger and explore my new environments, being aware of my pledge for research, but I was more like a child being seduced by the vibrant world surrounding me than a researcher. Wherever I looked I saw new patterns emerging creating an infinity of finely woven objects.
>
> I was aware of the presence of the light, my silent witness and guarding parent all the time, waiting patiently for me to follow it home into its very heart. Each time I called it appeared, reliably and joyfully, and each time revealing a new and thrilling aspect yet unchanging, reassuring me of its eternal companionship.

Most recently, in 2012 Frederick Aardema, a Canadian clinical psychologist, released *Explorations in Consciousness*.[57] This contains some fascinating insights into encounters in the 'personal field' with aspects of his own psyche that can present themselves as entirely independent entities. In particular he reports that any less developed aspects of the self can behave in a manipulative or even destructive manner, although in as much as they correspond to the 'trickster' archetype they can act as important conduits to personal transformation and enlightenment. More relevant for our current purposes are his comments on guides and higher selves:

Guides and higher selves are often given special status in the out-of-body literature as independent entities that exist apart from the projector. They are typically believed to function as 'helpers' that assist both the living and the dead. In most instances, however, you are having an encounter with *an aspect of yourself* rather than any sort of independent entity. They do not exist entirely apart from you. This does not diminish the value of such encounters. Guiding aspects are usually wiser and more intelligent than you are on any conscious level.

After going on to describe a reunion with his higher self involving 'joy and bliss unlike anything I had ever experienced before', he makes the following general observations:

An encounter with your higher self is almost always uplifting and inspirational. It tends to go far beyond what you know yourself to be. Even so, your higher self is a part of you, and encounters are still influenced by your own personal symbols and even daily preoccupations. Yet, none of this changes the value of such experiences, especially since the depth of the inner self is currently unknown.

In conclusion, we've seen that many of the modern OOB pioneers support the idea that *most* guides, helpers or other similar entities they come across during their explorations are merely other aspects of what they refer to as their own higher self or oversoul. We have also seen that to varying degrees most of those quoted in this chapter could be argued to show support for the concept of a broad, powerful and divine supersoul consciousness of which each of us are individual projections.

Indeed we can summarise the last three chapters into the first of the three fundamental precepts of Supersoul Spirituality:

each of us is a god in our own right...

5

TIME, CONCURRENT LIVES AND THE LAW OF ATTRACTION

...in which things will necessarily become a little more complicated. First we'll attempt to establish some basic rules about how time operates in the different planes, before moving on to the implications thereof, particularly in terms of re-evaluating the whole issue of reincarnation and multiple lives. We will conclude with a look at how all this dovetails with the universality of the law of attraction.

A SPIRITUAL VIEW OF TIME

From a historical perspective Eastern philosophies have always regarded time as a somewhat artificial construct, and this view is found in certain of the Western esoteric texts too. For example in the *Hermetica* we find that 'it is for the sake of body that place and time and physical movement exist'.[1] Similarly Plato asserts:[2] 'We use such expressions as what is past is past, what is present is present, what is future is future, and what is not is not, none of which is strictly accurate.' These sentiments are regularly echoed in contemporary channelled material too, for example by Gildas and Neale Donald Walsch's source:[3]

Your past, present and future do all exist in our dimension of time, and the moment of occurrence matters not at all. Ultimately they are all integrated. In doing this work too few of you realise how negligible time, as you know it, really is.

There is no time but *this* time. There is no moment but this moment. 'Now' is all there is. Everything that ever happened, is happening, and ever will happen, is happening right *now*.

These two are backed up by a number of channelled sources we've not met so far:[4]

You cannot disconnect your past, present and future, for they are all one.

There is no such thing as past and future, there is only *now*.

Time is a creation of the mind. Without the mind, time does not exist. In your dimension time, space, and movement are three separate elements of reality. When humanity reaches a higher degree of consciousness and with it an extended dimension, time, space, and movement begin to integrate more and more, until they become one. However, it is an error to believe that the next higher dimension is timelessness. There are many extended 'times', if I may use this expression, in the higher realms of being, long before you reach the state of being that is timeless... Time is at the disposal of human beings so that they can grow, fulfill themselves, experience, and reach happiness and liberation up to the limit commensurate with this dimension.

The past was simply a Now moment that was experienced and is no more... There is only the Isness of this Now. What is important is now. You are the product of Now. Your life is lived in the Now. Your future is created in the Now.

So it would appear that our perception of time as a continuous flow moving *from* the past, *through* the present and *into* the future is merely something we humans have developed to allow us to make sense of the physical world. Apart from anything else, with so much information flooding our senses and so great a desire to analyse it all, the ability to file away 'past' events is what stops us from simply frying our brains. But this perception of continuous flow is only that, a *perception*. What, then, is really going on?

THE FLUIDITY OF SPACE-TIME

We all know that some days time seems to fly, while others it seems to string itself out to such an extent that each minute takes an eternity. So, however much we rely on a standardised 24-hour day to give ourselves a consistent framework, we also know that our experience of time, even in the earth plane, can be extremely subjective. As with so many things in our apparently physical world, it's all about perception.

To understand what lies behind this idea that time isn't a fixed constant we must understand some fundamental physics.[5] One major breakthrough of Einstein's special theory of relativity was his demonstration that the Newtonian concept of absolute and independent space and time dimensions, which were previously assumed to act as a stable and dependable backdrop for all events, was fatally flawed.

Of course this runs counter-intuitive to our everyday experience, where events *do* appear to happen at a certain time and in a certain place. Yet most of us can also appreciate that when astronomers look out into space through powerful telescopes it takes a long time for the light from distant events, such as the formation of galaxies or the collapse of stars, to reach them. In other words they're seeing events that all appear to be happening now, but in fact span the whole spectrum of time since the universe was first formed. From this we can easily appreciate that time is in fact relative to the spatial coordinates of the observer.

Indeed relativity comes into play not only when huge distances are involved, but also huge velocities. So Einstein showed that space and time measurements must be made relative both to the observer and to each other, and that we must therefore consider space-time as a four-dimensional continuum. He also made it clear that space-time references or coordinates are merely artificial constructs used by an observer to describe their environment.

Einstein went on to extend his work into the general theory of relativity by bringing in the Newtonian concept of gravity. He showed that the gravitational force exerted by massive bodies such as planets and stars has the effect of bending or curving the three-dimensional space around them. This may best be conceived by considering how the rules of Euclidian geometry – which allow us, for example, to accurately draw a square on a two-dimensional plane by marking off right angles – no longer apply on the surface of a three-dimensional sphere. In the same way, gravity warps the space around a massive object so that normal three-dimensional geometric laws no longer apply – because the fourth dimension of time is also warped in the locality of massive objects. This in turn means that time can be seen to flow at different rates in different parts of the universe.

Astrophysicists weren't able to study black holes during Einstein's lifetime, but they provide one of the finest examples of warped space–time. They are formed when extremely large stars collapse in on themselves, matter being sucked into an increasingly small space in which it becomes ever more compacted. As a result they exert a massive gravitational attraction, which is what causes them to exponentially suck in any matter that strays into their vicinity. The effect of this huge gravitational field is to slow time to the point that, inside the 'event horizon', not even light can travel out and escape – so that from the external observer's perspective time has come to a complete halt. This despite the fact that theoretically, for anything that could survive within the black hole, time would be carrying on as normal.

SPACE-TIME IN THE HIGHER PLANES

All this serves to show us, from an objective, scientific perspective, not only that space and time are related to each other but also that nothing about them is constant even in our 'physical' universe. So how is space-time perceived in the higher planes?

TIME, CONCURRENT LIVES AND THE LAW OF ATTRACTION

One of the main factors that makes things appear to take time in our plane is the relative slowness of our movement. But what if you could speed up your ability to move about to the point that you could be anywhere else instantaneously, just by *thinking* about being there? Of course this is exactly what many OOB pioneers report when their consciousness is freed from the constraints of this plane. Here, for example, is Stylianos Atteshlis:[6]

> Since we live in the material world, in order to change our surroundings we must in some way move our bodies. In the psycho-noetical worlds, where no material body exists, our moves from one situation to another happen with the speed of thought. Change of environment, therefore, in the psychic world happens in a different way... For example, in the material world we move about on foot or in various machines. In the psychic world, movement takes place by thought and concentration. Anyone who has the ability to escape from the confines of the material body... can find himself travelling from one side of the planet to the other in a second or two... Conventional perceptions of time and space collapse.

So is there any sense of time at all in the higher planes? Well, why don't we find out from people who actually inhabit them – departed spirits themselves. One channelled source I'm particularly fond of, not least because of its searing self-examination and lack of ego, is the *Post-Mortem Journal* of no less a figure than TE Lawrence – of Arabia fame. This little-known gem was channelled by the British medium Jane Sherwood in the 1950s, and dictated via automatic writing. This is his description of how his experience of time changes as he progresses:[7]

> The sense of duration, which is each individual's measure of passing time, is checked and regulated on earth by exterior standards set according to earth movements and position with regard to the sun, hence time is a highly formalised concept which over-rides the individual sense of duration. Here the exterior checks are absent and we begin to realise that our sense of duration is a function of our kind of consciousness and

alters as the scope of that consciousness widens. In other words, the rate of experiencing quickens as we as ascend, and so the change over from time to timelessness comes about gradually as we are fitted to adjust to it.

My experience here has already shown me the beginning of this gradation. Up to the present – and you must remember that I have not yet progressed far – I have reached a stage of consciousness where I am aware of a great difference between my rate of living and the tempo of all my activities and those of men still on earth. Granted that men vary in their tempo even on earth, but taking one's experience in working with a medium as a guide, I find that I can only with difficulty slow down my rate to work with a mind still subject to earth conditions. It is tedious and fatiguing and sometimes I think nearly impossible, but it can just be done.

Another of Sherwood's sources, who has progressed further and is referred to only as 'EK', echoes Lawrence but introduces the fact that both space *and* time effectively expand as we progress through the planes – which is why those in higher realms hold awareness of a much broader span:[8]

The sequence of states of consciousness flows quietly by gathering still more of the future into the present. There is a lucid flow of being which alters one's sense of duration and adds beauty to the mere passing of time as it collects to itself the lovely future and passes it into the still lovely past... Each plane shows this contraction effect for space-time values... So it amounts to a progressive enlargement of experience. Thus each plane should provide a vantage ground in regard to those below it. From the higher, one should be able to survey a larger area of time and space in the lower.

So if there's still a sense of elapsed time in the higher planes, even if it's different from that in ours, is there still a sense of events occurring in some sort of *sequence* as well? According to OOB pioneers, yes. Here, for example, is Robert Monroe:[9]

Time, by the standards of the physical world, is non-existent.

There is a sequence of events, a past and future, but no cyclical separation. Both continue to exist coterminously with now... This is a state of being where that which we label thought is the wellspring of existence... As you think, so you are.

To sum up what we've learned so far, although we continue to experience elapsed time in the higher planes and there remains a sense of cause and effect, the perception of 'past' and 'future' is quite different. How can this be?

Peter Richelieu was another OOB explorer who worked closely with a guide, and in his 1953 book *A Soul's Journey* the latter provides an excellent analogy to help explain this conundrum:[10]

Past, present and future are in reality one. Let me give you a physical plane example to illustrate this. Imagine for a moment a river that twists and turns every few hundred yards. A man stationed on the deck of a river steamer... can only see that stretch of river in which the steamer is sailing at the moment... Let us suppose that another man is taking the same route in a helicopter; he would see the whole course of the river in one long sweep... To this man the scenery that the steamer has passed is just as visible as the scenery which meets the eyes of the passengers at the present moment, or that such people will see in the near future. To him there is no past and no future; all is indeed the present.

VERTICAL NOT HORIZONTAL TIME

To take this discussion a stage further, in 1969 Sister Frances Banks provided some interesting input when, via Helen Greaves, she reported that 'each moment holds in itself all of the past and all of the future'.[11] Since that time many books have been published containing the wisdom of supposedly higher entities – for example Gildas, Seth, Michael, Walsch's God and so on – but the practice of channelling ordinary people like Banks who have passed over relatively recently, which was so popular up to that point, has all but died out. All that remains is the continued use of mediums to pass on personal messages to loved ones in spiritualist circles.

However, thankfully there are several channelled sources we haven't yet discussed who have completely defied this trend in the new millennium, and for our current purposes the most important is Erik Medhus. In 2009, having suffered from severe bipolar disorder throughout his teens, he shot himself in the family home in Houston, aged just twenty. Some time after the initial shock his mother Elisa started to accept that he was trying to communicate with her, and began her 'arduous journey from sceptical physician to a believer without so much as a shred of doubt'. She set up the *Channelling Erik* blog and wrote about her experiences in her 2013 book *My Son and the Afterlife*. More important for us is Erik's own memoir, *My Life After Death*, which was channelled through the medium Jamie Butler and came out in 2015. In this he repeatedly discusses how things happen simultaneously rather than in a linear fashion, and adds:[12] 'Every moment is stacked on top of each other, not laid out in a straight line.'

These comments are useful but still leave our human understanding floundering somewhat. To help us further, some of the most fascinating and insightful comments about the true nature of time come from Charles Leadbeater:[13]

> What we call our past is not irrevocable, but is constantly changing, though always in the direction of improvement, or evolution. It may be said that the events of the past cannot be changed; but that statement is after all an assumption. The important events of the past are our contacts with other egos, our relations with them; and these relations are being changed, whether we know it or not; for they are in this direction at right angles to what we call time, which at present we are unable to appreciate.

He then adds a quote from Madame Blavatsky:

> 'Time' is only an illusion produced by the succession of our states of consciousness as we travel through eternal duration... The present is only a mathematical line which divides that part of eternal duration which we call the future, from that part which we call the past. Nothing on earth has real duration...

And the sensation we have of the actuality of the division of time known as the present, comes from the blurring of the momentary glimpse, or succession of glimpses, of things that our senses give us, as those things pass from the region of ideals, which we call the future, to the region of memories that we name the past...

No one would say that a bar of metal dropped into the sea came into existence as it left the air, and ceased to exist as it entered the water, and that the bar itself consisted only of that cross-section thereof which... coincided with the mathematical plane that separates... the atmosphere and the ocean. Even so persons and things which – dropping out of the 'to be' into the 'has been', out of the future into the past – present momentarily to our senses a cross-section, as it were, of their total selves, as they pass through time and space (as matter) on their way from one eternity to another.

All these reports appear to be hinting at something that Walsch's source finally makes explicit by talking about 'vertical' as opposed to 'horizontal' time:[14]

'Time' is not a continuum. It is an element of relativity that exists vertically, not horizontally. Do not think of it as a 'left-to-right' thing – a so-called time line that runs from birth to death for each individual, and *from* some finite point *to* some finite point for the universe. 'Time' is an up-and-down thing! Think of it as a spindle, representing the eternal moment of now. Now picture leafs of paper on the spindle, one atop the other. These are the elements of time. Each element separate and distinct, yet each existing *simultaneously with all the others*. All the paper on the spindle at once!

What are we to make of all this? Perhaps like me you feel you're close to a breakthrough in understanding but it's not *quite* falling into place. If so let me attempt to clarify with some ideas that came to me only after I'd thought about this a lot more. The suggestion from Blavatsky that time is 'a succession of states of consciousness' or 'glimpses', and from Walsch's source that it's 'not a continuum', are key points to grasp. Remember also that our perception of time as a continuous *flow* is only that, a perception. So how should we see it instead? I would suggest that we need to completely reconfigure our understanding as follows: *time is a series of discrete snapshots of an eternal now that encompasses everything that we perceive as the past and future, but is nevertheless forever changing from now-moment to now-moment.* This is surely what Walsch's source means when they reveal that 'the eternal moment of now is forever changing'.[15]

To help us understand this better, let's build on the idea that these discrete snapshots are 'vertical pieces of paper on a spindle'. Instead think of an abacus turned on its side, where each bead represents a complete record of the entire state of the universe at a given 'now-moment'. On each vertical string of beads, the central one represents the current now-moment. The beads below represent the snapshots of all the 'previous' now-moments, or the 'actualised past'. The beads above it represent the snapshots of the most probable state of the entire universe at each successive now-moment, which haven't actually happened or been actualised yet – so the 'projected future'.

If you think of our universe as a giant computer simulation or virtual reality game – an idea we'll return to in the next chapter – you can readily conceive that these projections are based on the recorded history of all the known choices made by all conscious entities to date, and their most likely choices and interactions that will lead on from this. But of course this future isn't predetermined because all entities have free will when making choices, and when they make unexpected choices – perhaps breaking old patterns of behaviour, for example – the actuality diverges from the previous probability. Then a degree of recalculation of 'future' probabilities is required, depending on how far-reaching are the effects of the unexpected choices.

All this is shown in the diagram. As we move forward/right one discrete time unit, say from t_{10} to t_{11}, t_{10} drops down one 'row' on the next 'column' because it's been actualised and therefore added to the memory store as a fixed reference point. Meanwhile the set of probabilities that were represented by $t_{11}@t_{10}$ – that is the most likely state of the universe in now-moment t_{11} as projected at t_{10} – are now being replaced by the actualised state at t_{11}. By the same token the set of probabilities $t_{12}@t_{10}$ have also moved down one and to the right to become the revised set of probabilities for $t_{12}@t_{11}$, which are now only one time unit away from being actualised – or not, depending on the choices actually made between t_{11} and t_{12}. And so on *ad infinitum*.

t_n

projected 'future'

$t_{15}@t_{10}$	$t_{16}@t_{11}$	$t_{17}@t_{12}$	$t_{18}@t_{13}$	$t_{19}@t_{14}$	$t_{20}@t_{15}$	$t_{21}@t_{16}$	$t_{22}@t_{17}$	$t_{23}@t_{18}$	$t_{24}@t_{19}$
$t_{14}@t_{10}$	$t_{15}@t_{11}$	$t_{16}@t_{12}$	$t_{17}@t_{13}$	$t_{18}@t_{14}$	$t_{19}@t_{15}$	$t_{20}@t_{16}$	$t_{21}@t_{17}$	$t_{22}@t_{18}$	$t_{23}@t_{19}$
$t_{13}@t_{10}$	$t_{14}@t_{11}$	$t_{15}@t_{12}$	$t_{16}@t_{13}$	$t_{17}@t_{14}$	$t_{18}@t_{15}$	$t_{19}@t_{16}$	$t_{20}@t_{17}$	$t_{21}@t_{18}$	$t_{22}@t_{19}$
$t_{12}@t_{10}$	$t_{13}@t_{11}$	$t_{14}@t_{12}$	$t_{15}@t_{13}$	$t_{16}@t_{14}$	$t_{17}@t_{15}$	$t_{18}@t_{16}$	$t_{19}@t_{17}$	$t_{20}@t_{18}$	$t_{21}@t_{19}$
$t_{11}@t_{10}$	$t_{12}@t_{11}$	$t_{13}@t_{12}$	$t_{14}@t_{13}$	$t_{15}@t_{14}$	$t_{16}@t_{15}$	$t_{17}@t_{16}$	$t_{18}@t_{17}$	$t_{19}@t_{18}$	$t_{20}@t_{19}$

t_0 — t_{10} t_{11} t_{12} t_{13} t_{14} t_{15} t_{16} t_{17} t_{18} t_{19} → t_n

actualised past

t_9	t_{10}	t_{11}	t_{12}	t_{13}	t_{14}	t_{15}	t_{16}	t_{17}	t_{18}
t_8	t_9	t_{10}	t_{11}	t_{12}	t_{13}	t_{14}	t_{15}	t_{16}	t_{17}
t_7	t_8	t_9	t_{10}	t_{11}	t_{12}	t_{13}	t_{14}	t_{15}	t_{16}
t_6	t_7	t_8	t_9	t_{10}	t_{11}	t_{12}	t_{13}	t_{14}	t_{15}
t_5	t_6	t_7	t_8	t_9	t_{10}	t_{11}	t_{12}	t_{13}	t_{14}

t_0 *succession of discrete, ever-changing, eternal now-moments*

Hopefully this provides some useful insight into the underlying workings of time, and gives us a clearer view of what Walsch's source means by the comment:[16] 'In many ways, life is like a CD-ROM. All the possibilities exist and have already occurred. Now you get to select which one you choose to experience.'

REINCARNATION REVISITED

To shift the narrative to a different but related subject, the *fourth* major shock to my spiritual system came *after* I'd developed the initial idea of the supersoul. As we saw in the opening chapter, the concept itself had already made me start to re-evaluate many aspects of the reincarnation-based worldview I'd spent many years establishing. But now I was being forced to confront the very *fundamentals* on which it was based – such as the notion of 'growing' across multiple lives one after another, and of an interlife between each one. As painful as it was I knew I *had* to follow this new evidence wherever it logically led, and that no longer could I avoid its more inconvenient elements.

The major element of this re-evaluation involved facing up to problems with the evidence about what happens after death that I'd previously just swept under the carpet. Now, as I read through a huge number of both channelled and OOB accounts of the afterlife that would go on to form the material for volume three of this series, I simply couldn't escape what was staring me in the face. It became abundantly clear that we don't merge with some sort of higher self not long after passing to the other side, and as a result suddenly become 'enlightened' and have access to memories about all our past lives and so on. Instead it is absolutely clear, indeed one of the fundamentals of understanding the afterlife experience, that our individual earthly personality survives intact when we leave this plane, and continues to survive for some considerable 'time' – not just as we roam through the astral planes, but to some extent even when we progress to the mental too. Yes our perspective changes considerably when we make this latter transition, but even then we still continue to identify primarily with the person we were in the earth plane. This continues until we progress to the very highest realms – which I refer to the 'superconscious' and 'metaconscious' planes.

Also missing from all these first-hand accounts are other fundamental elements of the interlife experience, such as meetings with other members of our 'soul group' to plan our 'next' lives together. In fact most of us had always talked about how the interlife experience actually exists in the 'eternal now' – but without exception we had always glossed over this conundrum because it was too complex to understand. Of course this also meant its proper implications weren't followed, but now I was determined to change all that. In some ways this was particularly painful to me, given the huge personal investment I'd made in these concepts over the years. I even used to refer to myself as 'one of the world's leading authorities on the interlife'. But facts have to be faced, and if we're to retain our integrity we must be prepared to change when new evidence comes along.

Just in case this still wasn't enough to convince me to change, at the same time I was also discovering just what various wise channelled sources had to say about the concept of reincarnation and of consecutive lives. For example, as we might expect the inimitable Seth waxes lyrical that our traditional understanding is entirely wrong – and that in fact the many lives of our supersoul aren't lived one after the other, but *all at the same time*:[17]

It is not correct to suppose that your actions in this life are caused by a previous existence, or that you are being punished in this life for crimes in a past one. The lives are simultaneous... There is instant communication and an instant feedback system... One life is not buried in the past, disconnected from the present self and any future self as well.

When you think of reincarnation, you suppose a series of progressions. Instead the various lives grow out of what your inner self is. They are not thrust upon you by some outside agency. They are a material development, as your consciousness opens up and expresses itself in as many ways as possible. It is not restricted to one three-dimensional lifetime, nor is it restricted to three-dimensional existence alone.

What you understand of reincarnation, and of the time terms involved, is a very simplified tale indeed... Reincarnation, in its own way, is also a parable. It seems very difficult for you to understand that you live in many realities – and many centuries – at one time.

Reincarnation, as it is usually explained, in terms of one life before another, is a myth; but a myth enabling many to partially understand facts that they would otherwise dismiss – insisting as they do upon the concept of a continuity of time.

Actually I had read these comments in the Seth material a long time before, but of course the concept of concurrent or simultaneous lives is extremely difficult for us to understand with our merely human brains and perceptions – so like so many others I just swept it under the carpet. But now I was finding that a number of other wise sources were echoing his view. For example, here is Walsch's source:[18]

> Past, present, and future are concepts you have constructed, realities you have invented, in order to create a context within which to frame your present experience. Otherwise all of your experiences would be overlapping. They actually are overlapping – that is, happening at the same 'time' – you simply don't know this. You've placed yourself in a perception shell that blocks out the total reality.
>
> You are also living other lives – what you call 'past lives' – right now as well, although you experience them as having been in your 'past' (if you experience them at all), and that is just as well. It would be very difficult for you to play this wonderful game of life if you had *full awareness* of what is going on.'

Full awareness would of course mean that we would be able to fully appreciate and understand that the other projections of our supersoul – such as the Ancient Egyptian priestess, the Roman legionnaire and the medieval serf – are all still operating alongside us in the present. I cannot for one moment pretend I fully understand how this could be, and I suspect most of us would feel the same. But that doesn't alter the true, underlying reality being put forward consistently by these wise ethereal sources. To illustrate the point, another of these that I haven't yet mentioned is Elias, channelled by the American medium Mary Ennis. This is what he has to say about the 'focuses', or what I would call projections, of our supersoul:[19]

> You choose your focuses and project from essence

simultaneously. Therefore, all of your focuses are being accomplished within the now. It is only within your perception that they appear to be past or future.

What is more, despite being both a more recent and a less experienced source of information, Medhus confirms this view:[20]

Imagine that every incarnation on earth is represented by a book... All the books are stacked on top of each another. Humans have only enough conscious awareness to concentrate on one page in one book at a time. That's important because to have the human experience, you have to be in the now. You can't have your head scattered in all directions, diluting the purpose of the life you're living, but all your lives are happening at the same time.

Meanwhile some modern OOB pioneers seem to support the idea too. Here, for example, is Jurgen Ziewe talking about his experience of observing supposedly 'past' lives:[21]

What is fascinating is that the past-life event is not an experience like a detached memory or picture, but is experienced in a here-and-now environment with the same reality as if it happened in 'real life'. This throws our whole concept of time and space into question.

We encounter a similar view from one of Rosalind McKnight's helpers:[22]

All souls are living in all lifetimes in the timeless dimension, but are experiencing them from the time perspective as if they were happening one at a time. The whole spectrum of the self exists in the timeless dimension, while various aspects of the energy levels are experienced in the time dimension for reasons of growth and perception.

In *Afterlife* I discuss the idea that the illusion of choosing a next life and getting ready to reincarnate may be possible for some who fervently believe in it, provided they remain in levels of the astral plane that are still sufficiently influenced by space-time.[23]

THE LAW OF ATTRACTION

Expressed in simple terms, the 'law of attraction' is really little more than a restatement of the idea of 'positive thinking'. Put more formally, it's the idea that we 'attract' or 'manifest' our reality or experience of this world via our thoughts, beliefs, intentions, expectations and so on. It will come as no surprise that I'd come across it a long time before I started the research for this book. It would have been hard not to given how a plethora of titles like *The Secret* and related films such as *What the Bleep?* rose to such prominence in the Western spiritual scene during the first decade of the new millennium.

I was always attracted to the idea, even if I felt some of the portrayal of it as a get-rich-quick scheme was unduly simplistic. Indeed, with so many authors making unrealistic promises to sometimes desperate people, and glossing over the intricacies of how the law actually works, they ran the risk not only of discrediting the whole notion, but also of seriously damaging already vulnerable people.

To be clear on this point, the reason we can't simply manifest our heart's desire – be it a new partner, car, home or whatever – purely using visualisation, mantras, vision boards and so on, is that our subconscious programming has a disproportionate influence on what we attract into our life. Moreover a great many of us experience difficult childhoods where the idea we're not good enough to be happy or wealthy, or not loveable enough to deserve a loving partner, and so on and so forth, are drummed into us incessantly. Guess what? The mud sticks! It doesn't matter what we chant or visualise with our conscious mind, if the tape in our subconscious is playing exactly the opposite tune over and over again, and has been for most of our lives, it will override any conscious desire. Until, that is, we reprogram our subconscious.

This isn't intended as a detailed treatise on the law of attraction – that's the aim of volume two of this series, *The Power of You*. For now it's enough to understand that it lies at the heart of another conundrum I'd previously swept under the carpet. How could we plan our next lives in sometimes great detail, yet still be using the law of attraction to influence our experience of this reality as we go along? Surely any pre-agreed plans might massively restrict our ability to manifest whatever we desired? The way I tried to resolve this was by claiming that our next-life plans represented a set of 'major probabilities and more minor possibilities', and that we always had complete free will to over-ride them. But, of course, once we recognise that all lives are happening at the same time, and there's no such thing as next-life plans, the conundrum disappears.

For anyone struggling with the fundamental ideas of the law of attraction, at the beginning of chapter 4 I described the 'thought-responsiveness' of the other dimensions, particularly the astral. All OOB pioneers and departed spirits emphasise this point. It lies at the heart of Monroe's insistence earlier in this chapter that 'as you think, so you are'. In other words, in realms not so subject to the restrictions of space-time, travel is instantaneous and pure thought can conjure up anyone or anything in the blink of an eye. What is more, who or what we attract isn't always pleasant, particularly in the lower realms. In this way the workings of the law of attraction are blindingly obvious in the astral.

Now in fact the same law underlies our earth reality. However here the constraints of space-time mean there's usually a delay between thought and manifested result. On top of that ours is a 'consensus' or shared reality, in which our own thoughts and intentions are mingling and sometimes competing with those of our fellows around us. This means the link between thought and manifested result is even more difficult to trace. Couple this with the fact that our subconscious thoughts and beliefs are often in conflict with our conscious desires and you have the recipe for a hugely persuasive illusion where it *seems* that things are happening *to* us. But they're not. Instead everything each one of us experiences is, one way or another, created or attracted *by* us. The implication of this is that, as all of the wisest channelled sources have been telling us for the last fifty years, the reality we're experiencing only acts as a mirror that projects our own thoughts and beliefs back to us. Of course this doesn't apply until we become adults and take on responsibility for ourselves, and it's also subject to certain restrictions that we'll return to in chapter 7.

The other thing to bear in mind when thinking about this law is the way almost all tops sports people now employ sports psychologists to help them visualise winning, and to 'keep them in the moment'. This is all about the law of attraction in action. But remember it applies universally – in other words it also operates to attract the *less* desirable things into our lives as well.

To summarise a somewhat difficult chapter, not only do we need to completely change our perception of how time works, but this in turn requires us to re-evaluate the traditional reincarnational 'truths' we thought were so simple and comforting. If all time is now, and all lives are happening at the same time in that now, then we simply must follow the logic where it leads – no matter how intellectually challenging it might be. The obvious implication is – pure and simple – there can be no such things as '*past*-life karma' or '*next*-life planning'. This means we need a completely different understanding of how the many other lives or projections of our supersoul interact with us, if at all. After all the universal constant of the law of attraction tells us that, even if they do exist alongside us, they cannot unduly influence the reality we experience – because this is something we attract or manifest via our *own* thoughts, beliefs and so on. We will return to these issues in chapter 7.

But now we can close this chapter by laying out the remaining two fundamental precepts of Supersoul Spirituality:

everything is happening in the now, and

the law of attraction reigns supreme...

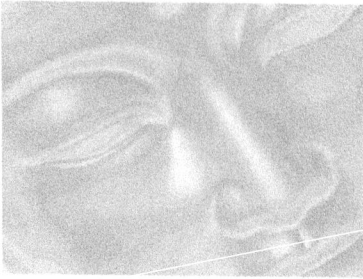

6

A DIGITAL UNIVERSE?

...in which things will become somewhat more complicated again. First we'll consider the possibility that the reality we're experiencing is only one tiny element of a massive digital game with almost infinite versions. Then we'll turn to the possibility of probable selves and of parallel worlds. It is important to understand that these ideas aren't fundamental to Supersoul Spirituality, so arguably this chapter could be skipped if one wanted to keep things simple. But arguably they help us to make a proper attempt at understanding the broader context in which our supersoul holographically projects aspects of itself into what are potentially a huge variety of multidimensional realities.

CAMPBELL'S BIG T.O.E.

One man has perhaps done more than anyone else so far to put together a complete, scientific picture of how the universe we're aware of only represents a tiny subset of a multi-layered virtual reality. A picture that takes us way beyond where even the most daring and open-minded of physicists and cosmologists would normally dare to tread. That man is Tom Campbell, a nuclear physicist by training who's also been having OOBEs for decades.

On a personal note, during the fateful meeting in the Indian cafe with Todd Acamesis described in the opening chapter, he began to sing Campbell's praises and the name rang a vague bell.

When I got home I investigated and found that a correspondent had sent me a link to Campbell's website back in early 2009. I then recalled that, just from watching his introductory video, I was so impressed by his description of a fundamentally digital universe that – and this is relatively rare for me – I put up a link on my own site. When another colleague mentioned Campbell completely out of the blue in a meeting shortly after this book began to take shape, I knew his work would be important in my new quest, even if at that stage I didn't know exactly how.

What I do know is that during one of those early discussions with Acamesis we strayed onto the topic of possible forgotten civilisations – and particularly ones that might have reached a level of cultural, spiritual and technological sophistication far in advance of our own. As usual I was dismissive of any such possibility. Why? Because this was one of my specialist subjects, and after huge amounts of research in my early writing career I found no *credible* archaeological evidence for the existence of either modern technology or modern human remains in remote epochs – and certainly not many, many *millions* of years ago.[1]

"Just hold on a minute," replied Todd. "What if there was an original digital 'version' of planet earth on which the human race did fully evolve in this sophisticated way? Perhaps evolution was accelerated somehow in that version so it all took place millions of years ago in our terms. Then let's say a decision was taken, by whoever created this game in the first place, to freeze that experiment, take a new 'copy' of the game and press the 'reset' button, taking it back to the point before even humanoids evolved, for example. This new version of the game is then allowed to run again, with maybe a few deliberately altered variables, to make sure it will play out in a quite different way."

My brain began whirring and started to overload. Every evaluation of different scenarios of human history I thought I'd made entirely rationally had been thrown up in the air. This was all seriously mind-bending stuff but, if it was essentially or even just partially right, *everything* would be possible and the sky really *was* the limit. What is more, when I finally got round to looking at Campbell's work properly, I found these were no idle claims.

It was at this point I discovered that Campbell has the remarkable distinction of having worked so closely with Robert Monroe in the setting up of his Institute that it was he and a close colleague, Dennis Mennerich, who introduced the 'binaural beat' audio system that would lead to the Hemi-Sync technology they now use.[2] It was also during this time at the Institute that Campbell's memories of having had extensive OOBEs from the age of five were triggered. In fact he recalled that they were closely guided experiences involving a variety of learning and tests similar to those Monroe himself had been through. They were brought to an abrupt halt by his guides at the age of eight, and over time forgotten, only for his extensive natural abilities to be rekindled some twenty years later – initially while learning transcendental meditation as a postgraduate lecturer and researcher, and then in vivid and highly evidential OOBEs shared with Mennerich under Monroe's supervision. After these three went their separate ways in the late seventies, Campbell embarked on a program of solo research over two decades that would culminate in the publication of his astonishing three-volume work *My Big T.O.E.* – or 'theory of everything' – in 2003.

To condense over eight hundred pages into just a handful will of course do Campbell's work no justice at all, especially given that I'm no physicist. If I start with the fact that in essence he proposes we live in a massive digital simulation, which can usefully be compared to the virtual reality of a giant, hugely complex, computer game, you get the idea. To make matters worse, like his mentor Monroe and all modern scientists he loves to use acronyms, while his style is to insert jokey and light-hearted interludes in amongst mathematical and scientific concepts and models that leave ordinary mortals like me gasping for air. Still let's attempt that summary because any set of theories that come from a man who, perhaps uniquely, combines a high level of expertise in both physics and OOB exploration, is likely to be both thought-provoking and hugely insightful.[3]

Despite their ultimate complexity, Campbell's models are actually based on just three fundamental and relatively simple ideas – and everything else flows from them:

1. *The fundamental building blocks of reality aren't matter but energy or, more accurately, consciousness.* This idea is hardly new. In fact it was commonplace among the most brilliant scientists of the early and mid twentieth century, but has taken more of a back seat amongst their seemingly materially obsessed successors.[4] Indeed Campbell and others of like mind would argue that it's the failure to understand this fact and shift to an entirely new paradigm that has thwarted their attempts to find the 'holy grail' of a unified and coherent 'theory of everything' that unites the macro level of relativity theory with the micro level of quantum mechanics. However the recent prominence given to the so-called 'hard problem of consciousness' – as in, where does it come from – places it back at the forefront of the debate.

2. *All consciousness ever wants to do is reduce its entropy (or degree of disorder).* Campbell also describes this as it wanting to improve its own 'quality' in terms of its 'level, breadth and depth of potential'. I would suggest we can perhaps paraphrase that it wants to evolve or grow by making itself more 'ordered'. Does that ring any bells? How about all the origin traditions from around the world that describe the initial attempts by the creator deity to create 'order out of chaos'?[5] But then it gets even more interesting – and challenging.

3. *Source is merely an undifferentiated 'primordial consciousness'.* Campbell makes it perfectly clear that under his model Source is not 'perfect love'. Indeed it has no emotions at all. It is simply a basic digital consciousness

that is always looking to grow, even if in the first instance that can only be achieved randomly and with no underlying intelligence. Just to hammer home the point he labels it Absolute Unbounded Oneness (AUO). Not everyone will agree with this postulation, of course. To be absolutely clear it was a huge culture shock for me, and one that took quite some time to digest. Talk about knocking down sacred cows!

Once we've recovered from this shock, let's see how the model unfolds. The first stage of differentiation is that AUO develops pairs of cells that are either in a uniform/non-distorted or a non-uniform/distorted state. Eventually, because from an evolutionary point of view the recognition of emerging patterns in these multiplying and interacting cells is a useful development, a computational and memory function emerges that he refers to as The Big Computer (TBC). Any evolving system is dynamic, that is it involves change, so another inevitable development would be some form of rhythm or clock that allows change to be monitored more intelligently. So time is invented relatively 'early' in Campbell's model and does underpin the experience of even the most fundamental states of consciousness. However it's not necessarily time as we know it, and it's definitely not tied in with space at this point.

These developments hugely increase AUO's options in terms of growth avenues, and it eventually evolves into the much more self-aware, organised, purposeful and complex consciousness of the Absolute Unbounded Manifold (AUM). AUM creates simulations in nonphysical-matter reality (NPMR) that allow units of individuated consciousness to experiment and grow, each simulation running in its own division or partition. But at some point AUM decides to experiment with a new partition on TBC called physical matter reality (PMR) that incorporates space as well as time, which will be an even more ideal environment in which individuated consciousnesses can interact and grow. So it develops a set of rules that will control this environment, most notably by *deriving* space *from* time by specifying the celestial speed limit of how quickly light can travel. From this we can see that space-time is a product of consciousness, *not* the other way around.

In terms of overall systems and subsystems, as far as Campbell can tell from his experiential observations while OOB, 'our system' is defined as encompassing a portion of our division of NPMR and our PMR – or the physical universe we inhabit and know about. But within NPMR there are numerous other PMRs that follow the rules of space-time, and any number of other subsystems that follow completely different rules.[6]

Some of the other most interesting aspects of Campbell's work are his thoughts on time, where we potentially find the full expression and explanation of some of its more difficult aspects. So, here we go...

In the last chapter I described how the eternal now changes from one moment to the next. In the accompanying diagram I showed how the most probable states of the universe projected for each of a succession of future moments are gradually replaced by what actually happened in each, these latter then recorded as the actualised past. I hinted then that if one thought of that model in terms of a computer simulation it might be helpful, and it will come as no surprise that it was Campbell's work that helped me to come up with what's hopefully a simpler and therefore more readily understandable version of his model of time.

So let's now look at how he takes this relatively simple model a step further. He suggests that the huge and, to all intents and purposes, unlimited processing power and memory capacity of TBC allows it to calculate and store not just the most *probable* state of our physical universe at any future now-moment, but also all those *possible* future states that are sufficiently likely and interesting to be *significant*. Note that in imposing this limitation he's massively reducing the amount of data processed and stored compared to the 'many worlds interpretation' of quantum theory first put forward by Hugh Everett in 1955. This latter insists that every single variation on a decision, no matter how small or inconsequential, isn't just computed but actually 'creates' a new, parallel universe – which is why it should be referred to more accurately as the 'infinite worlds interpretation'. I have always described such a theory as 'philosophically inelegant' – that is, wasteful and suffering from hugely diminishing returns if the overall context is for consciousness in all its forms to expand by gaining a variety of experience – and Campbell clearly agrees. However his explanation is far more scientific and derives from consciousness merely adopting the most efficient and 'profitable' – that is, lowest effort – solutions to its insatiable evolutionary quest.

The other factor limiting the size of the database is that multiple future possibilities and probabilities are only explored to the extent that they produce significantly different outcomes. As soon as any avenues start to converge, further calculation of options becomes wasteful and redundant. He emphasises that, although the definition of what constitutes 'significant' and so on would involve complex rules and algorithms, it's not so far removed from what human programmers already achieve in some of their more complex simulations using, relatively speaking, vastly inferior processing and storage capacity. Of course we're still talking about a huge database of information, far in excess of what we as humans can even conceptualise, but Campbell argues that the processes and calculations don't have to be perfectly precise or complete, just 'functionally adequate and statistically meaningful' – that is, good enough to efficiently assist the evolution of consciousness. He also insists that the database clearly *is* finite.

So how does adding in the significant possibilities change things? What we have now is that, at any given now-moment, what's usually one of the already calculated probable or even possible states will be actualised. If there have been seriously significant changes, as a result of free will being exercised in a way that's *dramatically* inconsistent with past behaviour, it's possible that a new set of calculations will have to be made – but this is likely to be relatively rare. Note also that a certain degree of randomness is inherent in an interactive, space-time based experience – indeed it's what makes it more interesting and flexible – but its impact shouldn't be overestimated, especially over longer-term projections.

Meanwhile what happens to all the data about the alternatives that weren't actualised? Is it discarded? No. All data about unactualised past probabilities and possibilities is retained. So even though limits are imposed concerning significance and so on, we have a massively full database just sitting there in NPMR waiting to be interrogated by anyone with the interest and the know-how. Welcome to Jung's 'collective unconscious', or what many others refer to as the 'Akashic records', and we'll return to their significance shortly. But note also that the database allows extensive what-if modelling of how scenarios would have played out had different decisions been made.

Incidentally, under Campbell's model the idea that consciousnesses in NPMR can exert a guiding influence on what happens in PMR is perfectly acceptable. So too is the idea that it's by learning to manipulate the probabilities on our personal timeline in the database, by intent and focused thought, that we develop the ability to consciously manifest our own experience in PMR. One of the main limitations on this, however, is the extent to which any outcome we might desire is tied up with any conflicting desires of others. The relative intensity of these competing desires will be reflected in their currently calculated probabilities, and if ours is significantly outweighed it will require focused effort to shift the balance in our favour. We can also see that it's generally easier to change the probabilities of something further away in time.

In terms of our fundamental theme, Campbell refers to the oversoul as 'our primary consciousness energy' that acts as a permanent retainer of the data and experiences collected by all the subsets it projects into various realities in PMR and NPMR.[7]

The good news is this sounds suspiciously like the supersoul. But what does he mean by 'various realities'?

PROBABLE SELVES AND PARALLEL WORLDS

Neale Donald Walsch's source states 'there's more than one of you moving down the timeline'.[8] Meanwhile anyone familiar with the Seth material will recognise the phrase 'probable selves' because he refers to them repeatedly. Actually Campbell quotes *Seth Speaks* as the closest model of how reality functions that he and Mennerich could find to 'tentatively and sceptically' work with, at least as a starting point.[9] This should perhaps come as no surprise when we've seen how Monroe went to visit Jane Roberts around the time the three of them started working together.

According to Campbell such references most likely relate to a version of you that already exists in the database of the probable future, or to a version of you that represents an unactualised past probability. He is at pains to point out that anyone who stumbled across this data, say in an OOBE, might run the relevant simulation and it would appear to them just as real as PMR. What is more the other people involved would appear to be making free-will-based, interactive choices, even though in fact they would just be simulations following the programmed algorithms predicting – albeit pretty accurately – their behaviour.

This is clearly one of the big traps that even quite seasoned OOB researchers can fall into because, unless you're extremely experienced and know exactly what you're doing – and not even Campbell himself would claim such a thing after decades of intense experimentation – you can be fooled into thinking that multiple, even infinite, parallel universes exist alongside our own. There are almost certainly some, as we'll shortly discover. But to the extent we're only talking about simulations, which will often be the case, these are *not* of the same ontology as the shared interactive experience of PMR that we collectively create in each now-moment, and which forms the actualised past. This is the only version in which we've collectively and *actively* used our free will.

The other versions held on the database are simulations that can only be experienced *passively*, however they might appear. This is another key distinction I've been emphasising for many years because it felt intuitively right, and it was wonderful to have it confirmed by Campbell.[10]

All this again argues against the infinite worlds interpretation. In the last section we saw that only *significant* possibilities are calculated, and now we can see that even these are just simulations – they do *not* create parallel universes that share the same ontology as the interactive, free-will experience we collectively create. It is worth noting that many worlds is the very interpretation of quantum theory pushed by those 'quantum mystics' whose desire to give spirituality some scientific credibility leads them to claim that somehow the existence of quantum uncertainty is what allows us to create our own reality.[11]

Experienced OOB pioneer Jurgen Ziewe similarly rejects the idea of infinite parallel worlds, despite his book's title of *Multidimensional Man:*[12]

> In my own experience the 'many worlds interpretation', although making sense from a quantum mechanical viewpoint, is in fact no more than a fantasy which falls short of the actual reality. It is simply that scientists try to explain nonphysical events from a physical angle and they end up with a misrepresentation of reality. To imagine an infinite number of versions of us, with googol to the power of googol combinations of events played out in an infinite number of universes, seems to me to be sheer madness. The universe does not operate on the laws of madness and it doesn't need to, because all experience it wants to explore it will, and to do this it does not need infinite copies of us or infinite copies of our physical universe.

There is, however, one important rider to the above. Campbell makes it clear that other PMR environments apart from ours *are* projected from NPMR, whether or not they form part of our system. What is more some of these may be spin-offs from our

PMR that AUM or someone else in NPMR thought would be productive alternative scenarios to explore in another partition of PMR, populating it with independent consciousnesses with free will. These could well be genuinely parallel worlds with a planet similar or even identical to earth, peopled with humans and so on. Moreover, although they'd be far from infinite in number, it seems our holographic supersoul consciousness might well choose to launch similar or even identical projections to us into such worlds too.

One example of this seems to be provided by British explorer Graham Dack in his 1999 book *The Out-of-the-Body Experience*. In this he describes an encounter with another English-town-type reality in which he interacted with a woman and her daughter for some minutes in apparent real time – only gradually realising she thought he was her husband arrived early for their rendezvous.[13] Much confusion ensued until he managed to get away and hide round a corner just before said husband arrived – who, it turned out, was almost identical to him in every way except wearing different clothes. Was Dack experiencing a mere simulation, or a genuine parallel life in another version of the earth game?

By contrast Monroe's multiple experiences of what he referred to as 'Locale III' involved him entering the body of a man who, as far as we can tell, looked nothing like him.[14] This was a physical environment similar to earth but the technology was quite different. For example, trains were powered by steam heated by what appeared to be some sort of nuclear process, cars were much bigger and slower, and there was no electricity at all. Worst of all, similarly to Dack's encounter, every time he took over the body of what he described as the 'I who lives there', confusion abounded with the man's wife – because all he had to go on were snippets of history gleaned from previous visits. However, unlike Dack's encounter, Monroe's Locale III seems very much like a genuine, parallel version of the earth game that has evolved in a different way.[15] Why was Monroe attracted to it? We can only assume that he and the man in question must have had some sort of special connection. Perhaps they were both projections of the same supersoul, possibly with some very similar traits? We will return to this idea in the next chapter.

To complete this discussion we should also note that there exist many versions of earthly towns, cities and other environments in the astral planes, but in Campbell's terms these are in our system's division of NPMR, not in PMR.[16]

Whether or not one accepts all of Campbell's Big T.O.E. – and he'd never suggest for one moment that anyone should do that as a substitute for their own direct experience – he does coherently present a complete, packaged alternative to a mainstream physics that often struggles to progress within essentially materialist limitations. He also provides a model of simulation-based probabilities and possibilities that's far more comprehensive and understandable than anything I've come across before. This man's brilliant and genuinely groundbreaking ideas deserve all the exposure they can get.

To close this chapter I'd like to quote his view of our obligations as humans:[17]

> Though the greater consciousness ecosystem is vast and ranges far beyond our view, there is much that lies within the reach of our direct experience and understanding. Humans have barely taken the first baby step toward knowing what is within our ability to know. As we continue to play our part in the larger consciousness cycle of entropy reduction, it is our right as well as our duty, to explore everything between where we are today and the far edge of our potential – to become aware and active participants in the Big Picture and full partners in the evolution of ourselves and AUM.

This more than anything tells us that his digital world should *not* be confused with the somewhat nightmarish scenario of *The Matrix* films, in which the dumb participants in the earth experiment are mere pawns being manipulated by a higher intelligence. The latter is not dissimilar to the extraterrestrial-plaything scenarios offered by various alternative researchers from Zecharia Sitchin to David Icke. Are we, the human race, helpless pawns? Or holographic projections of immensely powerful supersoul consciousnesses, and fully collaborating co-creators of our own destiny?

You choose which resonates best...

7

SUPERSOUL SPIRITUALITY

...in which we'll refine our new model by asking a number of questions, before laying out a new set of ten principles that underlie it, and closing with corroboration and further exploration from our sources of several of its key elements.

REFINING OUR NEW MODEL

To recap where we're at so far, if all lives are simultaneous and the life personality survives intact, the traditional reincarnatory idea that we have many lives one after the other in a linear progression of growth, in which the supposed lessons of one life are built into the challenges of the next, can no longer hold true. Instead we can think of ourselves as one of just many projections of our supersoul, all operating alongside each other while having experiences across all human eras and possibly in other realities too.

Using this as our starting point, let's now further refine our new model by asking a few pertinent questions that derive from comparing it to a more traditional version.

DO WE STILL HAVE MULTIPLE LIVES, AND IF SO WHO IS 'WE'?

Does the concept of having multiple lives still have any validity under this new model? The answer is only at the supersoul level. In other words if we can properly connect with and adopt the all-encompassing view of our supersoul consciousness, we'd gain an awareness of all our 'soul projections' and regard them as both individual consciousnesses in their own right and as full holographic aspects of ourself. But what about 'Ian', the human being I know and, mostly, love? Do *I* have many lives? The answer must surely be 'no', again unless I can genuinely adopt my supersoul level of consciousness, which involves appreciating that I'm far more powerful and multi-faceted than I would normally recognise.

A related implication if we don't have many lives one after the other is that the whole idea of 'addiction to the illusion' or gaining release from the 'wheel of karma', as discussed in chapter 2, becomes meaningless. In fact its proper context can now be seen to be addiction to the many sometimes-beguiling illusions of the astral planes after death, as we'll see in the final chapter.

'PAST' LIVES'... OR 'RESONANT SOULS'?
The question then arises, how and why do so many people – from those who seem to have momentary glimpses of other lives, to the full-blown experiences of regression subjects – identify so closely with what they feel to be 'their' past or even future lives, usually in different eras? My sense is that perhaps what they're experiencing is another personality with a closer tie than would be explained by making contact with just any other random soul belonging to the same supersoul consciousness – of which there could well be *thousands*. So what's the answer?

It seems likely that these closest ties are felt with those other projections of our supersoul who are facing similar challenges, or have similar emotional or psychological make-ups, or conversely can provide a strong contrast to our own experience. In fact, in just the same way that the supersoul creates each of us as a unique new mixture of traits – of which more shortly – it may well as a corollary create closer-than-normal energetic resonances between certain of its soul probes. Having said that, to some extent these may be automatically created by the similar energies. What is more those souls with whom we resonate most might *change* over the course of our lives as we decide to direct ourselves towards different challenges.

We might usefully coin a new term for these personalities with whom we're most closely linked, given that they're operating in a completely different context to what we're used to, and refer to them as 'resonant souls'. But it would still be misleading to think of these as 'our' other lives in anything other than the context of the entire supersoul.

DO WE, OR SHOULD WE, INTERACT WITH RESONANT SOULS?

We will consider how the supersoul *itself* interacts with its various projections at the end of this chapter. In the meantime the potential for psychic interaction between *ourselves* and other projections from our supersoul is almost certainly unlimited. The extent to which we actually *do* interact will vary, dependent not only on the degree of resonance we have with any of them, but also more generally on how open and receptive we are to their influence, and vice versa.

Different people will have different approaches as to the extent to which ties with resonant souls should be fostered. Some who are particularly open may gain great insights from some of them – perhaps particularly any 'future' personalities – during meditation and so on, which is obviously all to the good. Less receptive people will merely experience strong intuitions sometimes, and it'll usually be advantageous to be open to these even if their source is unclear. Nor should we lose sight of the favourable impact *we* can have on *them* by rising to and overcoming our own challenges. Incidentally, I'll explain why I'm still using the word *challenges*, and how they arise, shortly.

On the other hand any of us can sometimes find ourselves experiencing strong, *unhelpful* emotions that may make some sense in terms of our own life, but can't be fully explained and seem to be somehow exacerbated. Traditionally we'd have thought of this as past-life karma being carried over, but that no longer makes any sense under our new model. But they *could* at least in part be seen as stemming from the impact of resonant souls facing similar challenges but perhaps in a more intense form. In such cases we'd arguably do well to make a conscious decision to block them. In more extreme cases a sensitive person may be able to resolve such issues by making contact with said souls and even attempting some degree of healing. For others some therapeutic assistance to uncover their source may be appropriate, but probably more as a last than a first resort.

Above all, if we bear in mind the supremacy of the law of attraction as discussed at the end of chapter 5, I'd argue that there's a golden rule governing all of this. It is that each of us is fundamentally responsible for creating or attracting *our* own experience in each moment of now, which means the ongoing experiences of other souls — however resonant — are fundamentally *their* responsibility, *not* ours. Nor can they exert a strongly disruptive influence over us *unless* we believe they can and choose to let them.

IS THE IDEA OF KARMA STILL USEFUL?

Simultaneous lives automatically imply that any idea of 'past-life' karma is a nonsense. But does the idea of 'current-life' karma still have any relevance? The answer is a qualified 'yes', because this is really nothing more than the law of attraction in action. Of course we often tend to think in terms of how 'past' events have determined our current experience, usually incorporating a whole array of past associations along the lines of 'last time x happened, y was the result'.

Sometimes this is a useful evolutionary tool that keeps us safe. Learning that fire burns, for example. Yet we don't *have* to be governed by these past associations if they're unhelpful and we don't *choose* to be. At least theoretically a 'master of creation' should be able to invent themselves completely afresh in any new now-moment, by resetting all 'past' patterns and starting with a clean sheet — irrespective of the weight of 'past' probabilities they'd built up. We are not all masters yet but at the very least, rather than looking backwards, we can switch our focus to how what we're doing and thinking in the present will attract or manifest what we experience looking forwards. After all if you tried to drive a car purely by looking in the rear-view mirror you would struggle to direct it where you want to go.

All of this is discussed in much greater detail in *The Power of You*.

GOD, CHANCE, KARMA... OR 'BIRTH GIVENS'?

At the end of chapter 5 I mentioned the existence of some fundamental restrictions on the law of attraction. So what are they? This brings us onto arguably the ultimate question that almost everyone has pondered at some time in their life right down the ages: what is it that allows one child to be born into the worst depravation, poverty and squalor, with no love and possibly just abuse to condition their future responses, while another is born into a loving, stable family and enjoys all the privileges that money can bring? Well, clearly I'm not going to accept that it's the mysterious workings of a capricious god; nor blind chance. But nor can we rely on the idea of karma from a past life, or even pre-birth planning of this one, as we once might. So what is our new model's answer to this most fundamental of questions?

It is abundantly clear from pure observation that each of us *does* start with a very different set of potentials. I would suggest we should again coin a new term for these, and refer to them as 'birth givens'. These will encompass not only our own sex and main psychological, emotional and physical traits, but also the characters of our parents and other family members, their ethnicity, socio-economic position, geographical location and so on.

They will typically provide varying degrees of difficulty or challenge, but we shouldn't forget that certain skills and strengths, and propensities for expansive characteristics like love and compassion, will also be brought into the mix. Our childhood experiences – at least up to the point where we become largely responsible for our own lives and decisions, which varies for each individual – will tend to be so influenced by these birth givens that they should probably be thought of as part and parcel thereof too.

So who determines them? Under our new model they could surely only be chosen by the supersoul itself – although quite how it goes about this is an open question to which we'll return at the end of this chapter.

DO WE HAVE ANY SORT OF LIFE PLANS OR PURPOSES?

It seems then that we're here to 'paint the best picture we can with the palette we've been given'. What is more, especially when we bring in the idea of the supremacy of free will, it seems likely that any pre-birth planning of major events in our *adult* lives would be kept to a minimum. After all, once we remove the context of progression from one life to the next, what would be the point of the supersoul placing undue limitations on the experience of each soul projection? Under our new model the whole process of consciousness growing and evolving is inherently and hugely dynamic.

That having been said, is it possible that *some* major events in *some* people's adult lives don't just occur because they've attracted them in the ordinary course of events? This topic is at its most sensitive when we're talking about serious illness, even premature death, affecting ourselves or our loved ones. Rather than such events being planned *before* birth, is it possible that as adults we might sometimes make a *new agreement* with our supersoul to take on a new challenge? This would obviously be at a subconscious level, perhaps in our dream state, and one might argue that we'd attracted it to the extent that we'd shown ourselves ready to take on such a challenge. Whatever the underlying cause of such traumatic life challenges, the one thing we can say with certainty is that the people facing them have complete control over how they *react* to them.

So what about the related idea that each of us has a life purpose? This can't be completely discounted for some people, especially those who show a great talent and drive in one direction – for example, as an artist, writer, musician, sportsperson or similar. But nor, I suspect, should it be overplayed as if we *all* have one main objective in life that's planned in advance. Again this could only detract from our free will to follow *whatever* path we desire – and to change it, should we so choose, at *any* time.

Where, then, does that leave the related concept of 'soul contracts'? As with life planning, we can only conclude that use of these would be minimal – unless they were very much tied into birth givens, such as a child born with major physical or mental disabilities, for example. In this case it seems most likely that the challenges will have been chosen not just for the child but also its parents. In as much as there's nothing to suggest that our family or friends will be part of the same supersoul – indeed on intuition alone I suspect quite the opposite would normally be the case – this would imply that planning of challenges *between* supersouls almost certainly occurs on a reasonably widespread scale.

But, as with life plans, to take this idea of contracts too far is to risk the abrogation of personal responsibility for what we attract into our lives – and to cut ourselves off from our power to change our experience if we so choose.

HOW DOES ALTRUISM COME INTO PLAY?

The idea of the supersoul choosing serious physical or mental challenges as part of the birth givens for some of its projections brings us back to the whole issue of 'fairness' if we only have, effectively, one life. This is perhaps where our new model requires us to make one of the greatest perceptual leaps of all. Under traditional models we've tended to describe such lives as altruistic, in as much as that soul agrees to an especially challenging life not only for their own growth but also for that of others around them. What is more such a life has always been thought of as mitigated by other less challenging lives in that soul's reincarnatory chain. But of course none of this applies now. So what's really going on?

The rather beautiful fact is that under our new model arguably *everything* can be seen as altruistic – because everything that each soul experiences is designed to add to the databanks of the supersoul, thereby fulfilling its constant desire to expand its consciousness. From this perspective any particularly challenging set of birth givens, or any major new challenge accepted in adulthood, can best be seen in the context of 'taking one for the team'. We are engaged not only in an individual enterprise but also in a collective one.

From my own experience, the recognition that each of us can be characterised as 'a lead representative of team supersoul gaining experience at the coalface of space-time on behalf of the collective' really does have the capacity to alter the way we think. While it's not useful to lose our sense of individuality, this perspective potentially produces a whole different sense of responsibility. This despite the fact that, as stressed before, each of us remains fundamentally responsible for our own experience.

DO WE STILL RECEIVE GUIDANCE?

All the above would in turn suggest that, contrary to what we've been led to believe in the past, our supersoul consciousness – which, remember, is often confused with guides, angels and so on – is likely to exert minimal if any influence on us behind the scenes to 'keep us on our life path'. It also means that so-called 'synchronicities' are much less likely to represent 'guidance from outside' or unasked-for 'nudges in the right direction', and are much more likely to represent the sophisticated underlying dynamics of how our own creation and attraction process crystallises into our earthly experience.

Of course I'm not suggesting we *never* receive guidance or insights from our supersoul consciousness generally, or from wiser non-incarnate aspects of it, or even from other resonant souls who've passed a challenge we're facing with flying colours. But I'd argue that under our new model this would only come either as a result of us *proactively* requesting it, or because we *attract* it to ourselves automatically by our conscious and unconscious beliefs, intentions and actions.

WHAT ABOUT PLANNING ON A BROADER SCALE?

This brings us on to the whole issue of whether there's any

planning on a more 'macro' scale, and to that thorniest of examples – whether major wars and conflicts that impact so many lives are planned from other realms, or result from the excesses of a few aberrant souls?

The answer, it seems to me now, is neither. It is far more likely that, just as we create our own experience individually – often far more with our unconscious than our conscious minds – the same is true for us collectively. On that basis the accumulations of limiting and fear-based actions, beliefs and emotions of humanity as a whole would surely be more than enough to dynamically create mass experiences of war, depravation and, sometimes, utter brutality; and to do it more than once; and to keep on doing it because, for all that we've made some important progress, we're still a long way away from consistently choosing love over fear on a global scale. Then, as far as the individuals involved are concerned, the balance of probabilities, if they're born into a particular time and place where major conflict is likely, is just another factor in the make-up of their birth givens.

WHERE DOES ALL THIS LEAVE REGRESSION THERAPY?

It should by now be clear that any suggestion that something in our 'current' life can only be cured by healing the unresolved emotion from a 'past' one flies in the face of our new model. This is because any other lives are not 'ours' in any meaningful sense. Whatever human era they're based in, each one represents an ongoing, parallel dynamic with responsibilities of its own.

That's not to say that 'past-life' regression therapy can't still play a role. We've already seen that the other lives experienced might well be those of resonant souls with similar traits and facing similar challenges, or who act as a deliberate contrast. As such they might provide us with important insights into our own life, and any healing they receive as a result of regression might even help them and us to move forwards. But the fundamental rule is that they're responsible for their own experience, just as we are.

On the other hand it's commonly accepted among modern

regression therapists that supposed past lives experienced under regression don't have to be 'real' to have therapeutic effect. Nor is it beyond the bounds of possibility that guiding aspects of a client's supersoul might deliberately implant what might be entirely imaginary lives into their consciousness that again have important resonance and insights – thereby acting as a highly effective placebo to heal psychological damage suffered in this life that they prefer not to face directly because it's too painful. The only riders to this are, first, if the concentration on what are supposedly 'past' lives in any sense reduces the responsibility the client takes for the creation of their experience of their own life in the here and now; and, second, if the therapy relies in any way on fixed ideas of 'past-life' karma being passed on into their current life.

What, though, about being *progressed* forwards in time? Of course the visualisation of a 'future' now-moment in *this* life that's full of abundance and joy is an essential tool we can use *ourselves* in making the law of attraction work for us. Meanwhile any good regression therapist will use 'future pacing' to achieve a similar result. However when we come to the increasingly popular phenomenon of progression into an apparently future and *different* life, the same issues arise as with past lives. These aren't 'our' lives in any meaningful sense, and they're certainly not our responsibility – they're the responsibility of the personality who's *already* living them. So again we should make sure such therapy doesn't detract from the fact that our focus needs to be on creating our *own* unique experience *now*.

How, then, are we now to consider *interlife* regression? Our new model would suggest it can only be some sort of 'symbolic approximation'. But, if so, how is it that so many thousands of people have come to have what is often an extremely insightful and therapeutic regression experience? I indicated in the opening chapter that for some time I've regarded the modern body of material, collated since Michael Newton's work gained widespread exposure in 1994, to be relatively non-evidential because it's often unduly influenced by his blueprint. It is the earlier material from other pioneers, when the experience was less well-known, that might be considered as rather stronger. This was far sparser and less rigid, and the two elements that tended to stand out were the 'past-life review' and 'next-life plan'.

As far as the former is concerned, as I discuss in *Afterlife* it's a fundamental element of our transition to the other realms.[1] Having said that different spirits will undertake it at different times, and to some extent it's an ongoing *process* rather than a one-off *event*. In fact rather than it being a formal procedure perhaps overseen by some sort of guides or elders, as often characterised in interlife regression, for some departed spirits it appears more like an automatic by-product of the expansion of their consciousness once they're no longer in the earth plane.

That having been said, given the context of simultaneous lives, we've just seen that the 'past life' initially experienced by the subject to take them into the interlife would have to be either that of a resonant soul, or based on imagination, or a combination of the two. As for the reviews they experience, it's not difficult to make up material about how that personality might feel about that life, based on its main features. But nor can we rule out the possibility that, again, real guidance from the supersoul might be coming through at this point, if the challenges and traits of that other life – whether imagined or not – are shared. As for 'next-life' planning, by definition this is almost always for the current life, so under our new model it's hard to see this as being anything other than imagination mixed with an obvious, conscious knowledge of the challenges the subject's actual life contains – albeit that again interesting insights may emerge during this process.

It is interesting to note that similar reports of the interlife are encountered in some channelled material, particularly from Seth.[2] Given our new model we can only assume this was designed as a deliberate simplification intended to at least move our knowledge forwards from where it was under the traditional religions. In fact Seth more or less admits as much, at least about the concept of reincarnation, as we saw in chapter 5.

I have no wish to denigrate the usefulness of the interlife regression experience for those who choose to go down that path. Just as with past-life regression, even if it were only a highly effective placebo, if it provides important insights and helps people feel better about themselves that's great. As usual the rider to this would be if they're encouraged to develop a strong sense of having extensive life plans and contracts, which would detract from them taking responsibility and control in the now.

HOW DOES CHOOSING LOVE OVER FEAR FIT IN?

I have previously made brief references to this idea, which tends to be one of the basic principles of modern spirituality. So is it still just as relevant under our new model? Well, we've seen that consciousness always wants to expand itself, and in the human hologram at least expansion almost certainly implies coming from a place of love, while contraction involves coming from a place of fear. That is not to say that all experience – even a whole life dominated by greed and hatred, for example – isn't an important addition to a supersoul's databanks. But it seems almost certain that the ultimate aim for humanity as a whole is to allow love to predominate over fear even in the dualistic physical plane – or to create 'heaven on earth', because without doubt unconditional love is the prerequisite for progression to the higher afterlife planes.[3] The corollary is that as individuals this might be seen as a sort of overarching life purpose for all of us.

What are the implications of this? During any single day each of us is given multiple chances to choose a love-based rather than a fear-based reaction to all sorts of different circumstances – and we have completely free will to choose which way we go in any given situation. But it's surely the case that any action or decision we take from a position of love will resonate with this higher purpose because it's expansive, and will literally make us feel good inside. The opposite is equally true, so that any fear-based action or reaction will cause our energy field to contract. I also strongly suspect that the more we become aligned with this purpose the worse the physical effect will be – so that, for example, any burst of anger on our own part, or just in our presence, will literally *feel* unpleasant and even painful. That is certainly my own experience.

So, although I proposed earlier that life planning and guidance are kept to a minimum in our adult lives under our new model, this is the one area where I'd expect the higher aspects of our consciousness to try to exert an influence – by directing us down the path of love rather than fear wherever possible. Having said that, because of varying birth givens including psychological makeup and childhood experiences, there can be no doubt that in adult life some people will find it easier than others to choose and express love. Remember, though, that our aim is to paint the best picture we can *with the palette we've been given* – not the best picture ever.

In the interests of practising what I preach, for those who are interested I've attempted to apply our new model to my own life in the Appendix. This exercise reappraising areas such as life purpose, guidance, birth givens, soul contracts and interactions with resonant souls, by comparing my old approach and interpretation with the new in each.

A NEW SET OF PRINCIPLES

We have already developed our three new precepts of Supersoul Spirituality in the preceding chapters. To recap they are:

Each of us is a god in our own right

Everything is happening in the now

The law of attraction reigns supreme.

However we can now take the model somewhat further with a refined and more detailed set of 'ten principles':

1. We are holographic, expeditionary projections sent out by a supersoul consciousness possessing a wisdom and power of divine proportions. Myriad supersouls are involved in the

simulation game we call 'human life on earth', which is just one of myriad different realities they project aspects of themselves into.

2. After death we continue to identify with the personality of the life we just left, so this and the individual 'soul' are the same consciousness.

3. Although we're engaged in the expansion of consciousness, we don't develop in a linear fashion as we move from one reincarnatory life to another. Instead the lives of all souls projected by the supersoul are happening at the same time – even if they're operating in different human eras.

4. 'My' many lives means nothing unless we're genuinely adopting our supersoul level of consciousness, which involves appreciating that we're far more powerful and multi-faceted than we normally recognise. Any experiences we have of 'past' or 'future' lives are most likely those of other 'resonant souls' projected by our supersoul with whom we have an especially close connection – for example because of strongly shared traits or challenges, or because they act as contrasts.

5. Each of us is fundamentally responsible for creating our own experience in each moment of now. We are not limited by 'past karma', whether from this life or a supposedly previous one, unless we believe we are. Nor will other resonant souls tend to be able to exert a strongly disruptive influence over us unless we believe they can and choose to let them.

6. Our supersoul chooses our 'birth givens', and these vary considerably. They include our own sex, our main psychological and physical traits and propensities – in terms of both challenges and strengths – and the ethnicity, socio-economic position and geographical location of our parents. On that basis we're here to 'paint the best picture

we can with the palette we've been given'. Other than that any pre-birth planning of events in our adult lives, or 'soul contracts' with others, are probably kept to a minimum to give us maximum free will to direct our experience. It is also unlikely that most of us have a preplanned 'life purpose', because again this would tend to detract from our free will to follow whatever purpose we desire – and to change that purpose, should we so choose, at any time.

7. Angels and guides may well be other aspects of our own supersoul, and they won't tend to interfere with our experience on the basis that they supposedly 'know best' and 'want to keep us on our path'. Usually therefore synchronicities will only represent the sophisticated underlying dynamics of how our *own* creation and attraction process crystallises into our experience.

8. Having said that, insights and guidance are always available if we *proactively* ask for them, or if we *attract* them to ourselves automatically by our conscious intentions and actions. Such guidance might come, for example, from wiser, non-incarnate aspects of our supersoul, or from other resonant souls – perhaps even operating in the 'future' – who have overcome similar challenges. By the same token we can provide guidance to them by overcoming our own challenges, if they're open to it.

9. On rare occasions we might make a new agreement with our supersoul, at a subconscious level, to take on a new challenge in our adult lives. But it's always best to take responsibility for any challenge by assuming you created or attracted it, or at least by knowing you control your reaction to it. Any tendency to ascribe challenges to 'past' karma, life plans or soul contracts can lead to an abrogation of responsibility for what we're creating in the now, and detract from our extensive power to turn any situation around.

10. Under the supersoul model *everything* can be seen as altruistic, because everything that each soul experiences is designed to add to the databanks of the parent consciousness. Any particularly challenging circumstances or birth givens can best be seen in the context of 'taking one for the team', and each of us can be characterised as a 'lead representative of team supersoul gaining experience at the coalface of space-time on behalf of the collective'.

CORROBORATION OF OUR NEW MODEL

Several of our sources provide corroboration of our new, particularly in the two areas of how resonant souls interact with each other, and how birth givens may be selected.

INTERACTIONS BETWEEN RESONANT SOULS

If we start with our channelled sources, and forget resonant souls for a moment, Charles Leadbeater starts us of by raising the possibility that 'past' interactions within our *current* life aren't fixed — because in his comments on time quoted in chapter 5 I deliberately omitted the following extract from the middle:[4]

This transcendental view of time has been very beautifully expressed by the late Mr CH Hinton in his story *Stella*: 'If you felt eternity, you would know that you are never separated from anyone with whom you have ever been. You come to a different part of yourself every day, and you think the part that is separated in time is gone, but in eternity it is always there. If you felt eternity, you would know that what you did to a person and what he did to you is gradually changing. You think it is over and done with, but in eternity what you and he did to each other is always there and always changing and altering. As you grow better, he will act quite differently and you will act quite differently. If you felt eternity, you would know that you are always living in your whole life, that it is always changing, though with your eyes you can see only the part you are in now. The present is just a concentration, like attending to one thing at a time.'

The entity Elias expands on this by referring to interactions between what he calls 'focuses', which in our terms would be resonant souls:[5]

I do express often to individuals within this forum that all of your focuses are continuously influencing of each other and of this focus, as you also are continuously influencing of all of your other focuses. But your attention is in *this* focus, and your creations in this focus are *your* creations. They are purposeful, they are intentional, and they are the responsibility of this particular focus. Therefore, as you continue to direct your attention to this particular focus in which you hold your attention, you also empower yourselves much more and create much more of your own expression of freedom and your ability to manipulate energy intentionally within this focus. It offers you the opportunity to view *how* you create your reality, and that you *do* create your reality individually, that your choices are your choices. You hold free will. You are not subject or victim to *any* expression of energy within *any* area of consciousness.

In several separate quotes Seth then expands on this crucial idea that, despite any such interactions, each of us is in complete control of *this* life we're living *now*:[6]

[Your other] lives exist simultaneously. They are other expressions of yourself, interacting, but with each conscious self possessing the point of power in its own present.

Since all is simultaneous, your present beliefs can alter your past ones, whether from this life or a 'previous' one. Existences are open-ended... *The point of power is in the present*. This experienced present also represents your psychic touchstone to all of your other existences... All of your other 'reincarnational selves'... are unconsciously aware of your conscious experience, as you are unconsciously aware of theirs. The interaction is constant, however, and in *all* of your presents, creative. You draw on their knowledge as they draw on yours, and this of course applies to personalities that you would *consider* future. You have a gigantic pool of information and experience to draw upon, but this will be utilized according to your present conscious beliefs.

Within any given twenty-four hour period, then, traces and aspects of all your other experiences appear in their own way. You each contain aspects of your other identities within your current selves – some very obvious perhaps and others barely noticeable... The adventures of your simultaneous selves, again, appear as traces in your own consciousness, as ideas or daydreams or disconnected images, or sometimes even in sudden intuitions. They can be drawn upon, drawn out, to help you understand current problems. This does not mean that you will necessarily have a flood of reincarnational information, instant intuitive recognition of 'past' lives, or experience any such *intrusive* data. It does mean that in your own life such information automatically appears in intimate ways, but couched within the framework of your own comprehensions, even passing unobtrusively through your conscious thoughts... Impulses to try activities you have not tried before may indeed be messages from other portions of your own being.

Meanwhile Neale Donald Walsch's source again reinforces the idea that, despite these interactions, no other resonant soul can exert an undue influence on us unless we allow them to:[7]

No individual aspect of divinity has power over any other aspect of divinity. It is not possible for one soul to affect another against its will.

They also discuss how what we would think of as a 'future' version of our own life personality, presumably a 'probable self' in terms of the discussion in the last chapter, can come through to us via intuition:[8]

Have you ever had a 'strange foreboding' about some future event – so powerful that it made you turn away from it? In your language you call that premonition. From my viewpoint it is simply an awareness you suddenly have of something you've just experienced in your 'future'. Your 'future you' is saying, "Hey, this was no fun. Don't do this!"

Turning to our OOB sources, Frederic Aardema too discusses the potential part played by 'reincarnational or future selves' in providing inner guidance.[9] Similarly Jurgen Ziewe considers the possibility that 'we may already be the beneficiaries of our future selves, who can project themselves into any one of our past, present and future lives and assert a guiding influence if so chosen'.[10] But it's Gordon Phinn who discusses the idea of interactions between resonant souls in by far the greatest depth. In his second book he admits to a degree of confusion about the paradoxes of time when experiencing the expanded consciousness of the realms in which his supersoul or 'higher self' resides:[11]

> Then I move up to formless worlds of transcendent energies where Higher Selves dwell. Been here many times in meditation. Move into Higher Self and interact with other 'personality projections', those souls who, gladly or otherwise, took part in history. The whole notion appears of their lives being complete and their being 'permanent' residents of Higher Self, while I'm still doing my thing here and only visiting, and I juggle with it, as it seems to contradict the notion that all lives are simultaneous for Higher Self.

Elsewhere he asks to communicate with a 'future' self and tunes into Cassiopeia, who lives around 2150. He describes her as almost goddess-like by current standards, and how she takes regular trips back in time to visit 'previous' personalities. But it's in his third book that he really expands on these ideas. In particular, when he again attempts to tap into the broader awareness of his higher self, he absolutely corroborates my concept of resonant souls by describing a *subset* of personalities – selected from amongst the far greater number projected by his supersoul overall – that he most interacts with, despite the fact they're operating in apparently different human eras:[12]

> They are only a representative sample, the most influential and if you like habit-forming creatures in the available spectrum. As my grasp on Higher Self reality is as yet incomplete, perhaps I would be wise to say 'the most influential on Gordon'. I

certainly feel their repeated influence on his issues and choices, and I believe my psychic influence on them is something that will come up as we continue to explore. All the Higher Self projections put together might look like a mini-society, with every character type and ethnic trait represented. What I think you're getting here is a small clan within that group:

(1) Gordon; (2) James, a king; (3) David, a philosopher; (4) William, another philosopher; (5) a druid priest figure, c. 20BC - 30AD; (6) a Celtic chieftain of the middle ages; (7) a small time businessman in ancient China; (8) a wife and mother in ancient China; (9) a trader in Holland, c. 1600-1650; (10) a young girl, dead at around five, c. 1900; (11) an outcast, selling herself to survive, England c. 1730; (12) a wife awaiting the return of her husband from sea; (13) a wealthy and influential Venetian courtesan, c. 1550; (14) a member of the priestly caste under Akhenaton in Egypt; (15) the artistic son of a wealthy Athenian family, bisexual; (16) a lesser known member of the Neoplatonist school; (17) a contemplative monk in England, c. 1300; (18) an abbot of a monastery, c. 1400; (19) an Irish monk, c. 700; (20) a daughter of high birth, left pregnant while husband goes to war (1650?); also an archetype for... (20B), a young wife who lost her husband at sea, c. 1880; (21) a French noblewoman with an inherited estate, bisexual playgirl, c. 1780; (22) an Atlantean male, steeped in magical energy work, yet carefree and completely without the ego attachments of those who engage in the 'magical workings' of more recent times; (23) a woman and a man, fairly primitive, brutal 'Viking Raider' types; (24) a minor Scottish noble, impoverished, c. 1250; (25) a Buddhist monk (India/Tibet/ Nepal) c. 1000.

The following passage then provides us with a wonderfully detailed description of how his higher self is busy assisting various of these co-existing personalities in the eternal now:

Let's take a peek into what you would call the 'right now', so you can feel the transcendence of time and space that is 'my' almost constant experience. I am feeding Gordon (1) images and ideas. I am helping the king (2) come through difficult and delicate negotiations with himself and others over what he perceives as 'god', to arrive at decisions that will hopefully balance the various needs and desires of the warring religious communities under his care. I am feeding two male philosophers (3 and 4) mental energy to assist in their cogitations, although I do not attempt to impose any type of result. I am giving courage to the lonely, fearful wife (12) who fears she has lost her husband at sea. I am giving the courtesan (13) the perceptive power she needs to distinguish her appreciation of 'God' from her disgust of his selfish, grasping, power-addled servants on earth, while trusting that same energy might be used to corral and redirect some of her own vanities. I am offering the energy of courage to a number of soul probes involved in dangerous, perhaps life-threatening circumstances, including expectant and delivering mothers in situations where the risk of infection is high and the availability of competent medical care low... I observe the mosaic of energetic interactions between all my soul probes, as they feed and receive impulses from each other.

The way in which the real-time interactions between them occur is then described in wonderful and equally vivid detail:

As the king (2) worries about his wife, who has recently delivered but is still confined, the philosopher (3) considers the more human aspects of the kingly life, about which he is writing. The poor discarded wretch (11), made pregnant by her employer, wanders the fields and lanes of her rural territory begging for a berth and some employment; while the high-born maiden (20), romanced into her knight's father's castle, longs for his return, with babe in belly. The Dutch trader (9) awaits with trepidation the birthing of his second child, the ancient Chinese trader (7) looks forward to child number six, while the contemplative monk (17) simultaneously prays for the health and well-being of all the local children and gives thanks that he himself does not have to so cope; and the abbot (18) prays for guidance and forgiveness concerning the pregnancy of a nun he is particularly close to. As you can imagine, all their thoughts, anxieties, fears, joys and prayers come in my general direction and as I absorb, reflect and transmute them they become a small catalogue of possible reactions to an archetypal situation in human physical existence – and another contribution to my databanks of incarnate experience.

Now take that thought and apply it to, say, a simple expression, of frustration or impatience. Because of their varying energetic makeup each one of the above characters has a distinct experience and therefore expresses themselves uniquely, although each microsecond and each tiny shade of decision is influenced by all the other personalities. Singly they contribute to their personal drama, but collectively they embroider a many-hued pattern, a veritable encyclopaedia of impatience, whose details can be drawn on in the later stages of my, and our, ascension.

When the king (2) contemplates a decision of state, he draws upon not only his own decision-making abilities and the strength he draws in prayer from his 'god', but also all the decision-making abilities, and lack of them, in all the others in his soul group. And his eventual magisterial announcement will influence the many more quotidian decisions of the monks, mothers and sailors he shares his source with. Whether they know it or not, and most do not, each is of the other and they all gradually contribute their strengths and weaknesses to the advancement of the whole.

Phinn admits he was inspired by Bruce Moen's books, and it will be useful to close this section with the latter's description of his 'disk' – and in particular to how the other members thereof are intimately connected to him via a whole mesh of cords along which information passes:[13]

I, the one in my physical body, am nonphysically connected to members of the Disk via something that looks, to my perception, like a multi-strand, fibre optic cable. It connects between the shoulder blades and may be the basis of the 'silver cord' others have written about. Information passes through this 'cord' between myself and my Disk giving Disk members awareness of my activities and me awareness of them, once I learned how.

SUPERSOUL

THE CHOICE OF BIRTH GIVENS

First of all, our most recent channelled source, Erik Medhus, provides excellent, first-hand corroboration of my concept of the interplay between birth givens and free will as follows:[14]

> You don't choose to be born with a certain hair or eye colour... or a genetic predisposition for high blood pressure or addiction – but your soul does choose certain paths that you may or may not be aware of when you're alive as a human. Say a child is born in to a loving family but also grows up struggling with bipolar disorder, like I was and did. That's because my spirit chose to walk that particular path, and then as I lived out my life, I was presented with various choices I had control over that were influenced but not predetermined by my soul's path.

More broadly, though, we've seen that our birth givens must be chosen by our supersoul. But what we haven't yet discussed is how this is done. For example, are they based on combinations of traits from 'past' and 'completed' projections, or are they determined simultaneously for all as unique combinations? This is the way Moen describes the creation of each new projection by his 'greater self' or disk:[15]

> It is also my understanding that I was created by my Greater Self as a unique combination of traits of Disk members. My Greater Self used parts of itself to create the unique personality that I am. From one perspective, I see myself as a 'probe', not unlike something NASA would launch to explore the unknown. In other words, my Greater Self created me from parts of itself and sent me into physical world reality to explore.

There is a channelled source that we haven't discussed yet who comes up with similar ideas. For a long time I only knew Frank DeMarco as the co-founder and chief editor of the US metaphysical and alternative publisher, Hampton Roads. But around the time the idea for this book was first forming, a friend explained that he was an author in his own right and lent me a copy of his most recent book, *The Cosmic Internet*, published in

2011.[16] To summarise what is a sometimes complex narrative, his sources describe the idea of a 'group-mind' or 'family of souls' that sounds very much like the supersoul – also making it clear that there are seemingly endless higher aggregates of group consciousness above this, similar to Moen's endless disks. They add that 'new' souls are formed from a combination of multiple 'threads' or personality traits from 'past' souls within the group who have incarnated in human form. As human personalities we then have to act as 'ringmaster' for all these disparate threads, the purpose being to use our free will to get the most out of the unique hand – or combination of traits – we've been dealt.

Frederic Myers's suggests that we reincarnate but sparingly if at all, and seems to be hinting at the same idea in suggesting that each soul's karma is taken on by a new soul from the group:[17]

> I shall not live again on earth, but a new soul, one who will join our group, will shortly enter into the pattern or karma I have woven for him on earth – although no doubt 'karma' is a word I use incorrectly here, for it is something more and something less than karma that he inherits.

All this may help us to understand what may have been an original meaning underlying the Buddhist concept of *anatta* discussed in chapter 2. We saw there that what passes from one life to another via the rebirth process is regarded as a 'stream of consciousness' or a 'set of mental processes'. This emerges from the disaggregation that occurs at death, and it's also seen as contributing to a new set of five aggregates or *skandhas* that go to make up the new life.[18] These are now commonly and somewhat confusingly translated as 'form, sensation, perception, mental formations and consciousness', yet in the earliest Buddhist texts they were described quite differently as the 'various aspects of the way an individual manifests'. Is it going too far to see the similarity between this and what Moen and DeMarco's sources are describing? Would it even be stretching the point to suggest that our new model might just be the 'missing link' between Buddhism and more conventional reincarnation-based models?

Of course the doctrine of *anatta* was designed to force followers not to see themselves as separate from everything and everyone else, but to accept the interdependence and relativity of all forms – most obviously to help them to pursue a life of universal compassion. But again I'd suggest that we can see ourselves as individuals without having to see ourselves as separate. What is more this is very much in keeping with the collective, altruistic worldview that results from our new model.

Arguably this new model in which each of us forms part of a supremely wise and powerful supersoul consciousness provides just the sort of radical shake-up that is needed as we collectively pioneer huge changes in the earth plane, and perhaps finally move towards some degree of spiritual maturity. Surely it's time to move on from the sort of worldviews that have so far dominated the many thousands of years of humanity's recorded history – in which god, karma or pure blind chance determined our fate – and to replace them with something more sophisticated. More than ever before Supersoul Spirituality emphasises our personal *responsibility* for the experiences we create in our lives as we go along. But it's also a model of real *freedom* to direct our experience wherever we want it to go. A model that allows us to take real *credit* for challenges we successfully overcome. Above all, a model that emphasises the supreme creative *power* we all have, if only we choose to recognise this fact and use it.

So let us close by looking at the full implications of our new model...

8

WE ARE THE GODS!

...in which we'll examine the general, far-reaching and momentous implications of the introduction of the concept of the supersoul. Many of you have already begun to understand that you create your own reality, but are you ready for the next step? Are you ready to bask in the full glory of your supersoul? What extra power does this confer, and what extra responsibilities come with it? Why are more sophisticated models of soul consciousness now being revealed to the human race? Can they even play a significant part in moving us forwards and taking the next step in our evolution?

ACCESSING SUPERSOUL WHILE INCARNATE

Another researcher who's been working on the idea of simultaneous lives is the medium Julia Assante, whose book *The Last Frontier* was published in 2012. She suggests we should be looking to make more use of the knowledge and wisdom available from what she refers to as our 'oversoul':[1]

> The oversoul is far more than the sum of its parts. It organises individual consciousnesses, even giving birth to them. It is then our parent consciousness in a way. We are not lost in this massive superentity, nor are we diminished by it. I do not know enough about the oversoul but one thing is clear to me: it is an inconceivably vast resource of knowledge, inspiration and energy. If we were only more practiced in accessing it!

As for our channelled sources, having already introduced this issue in chapter 3, perhaps unsurprisingly Seth goes the furthest in indicating just how much wisdom, knowledge and creative power is available to us if only we open ourselves up to our true 'multidimensional self':[2]

> You have the knowledge of your entire multidimensional personality at your fingertips. When you realise that you do, this knowledge allows you to solve the problems or meet the challenges you have set, quicker, in your terms; and also opens further areas of creativity by which the entire play or production can be enriched. To the extent, therefore, that you allow the intuitions and knowledge of the multidimensional self to flow through the conscious self, to that extent not only do you perform your role in the play more effectively, but you add new energy, insights and creativity to the entire dimension.

However it should comes as no surprise that it's our OOB pioneers who have most explored these possibilities. To start us off, Charles Leadbeater describes the 'Buddhic' plane as follows:[3]

> To enter that plane at all is to experience an enormous extension of consciousness, to realise himself as one with many others... Yet in all this strange advance there is no loss of the sense of individuality, even though there is an utter loss of the sense of separateness.

Meanwhile Yram explains that each of us has the capability to expand into true divinity:[4]

> The further one penetrates into the more subtle states of matter, the further does this lucidity increase, to attain its absolute fullness at that point where our own universe contacts the Infinite, to which it gravitates. In this supreme state, man has become a god, fecundating his portion of the universe with the conscious life, of which he has now become both the centre and the circumference.

More recently Gordon Phinn's 'higher self' indicates just what power anyone who properly opens themselves up to their supersoul can access:[5] 'You are us and can have the accumulated wisdom of our data banks at your fingertips pretty much any time you wish.' Meanwhile one of the finest accounts of a full merger with one's fellow projections comes from Robert Monroe when he enters the realms of the INSPECs, which we briefly referred to in chapter 4 but can now fully appreciate:[6]

> I am in a bright white tunnel and moving rapidly. No, it is not a tunnel, but a tube, a transparent, radiating tube. I am bathed in the radiation which courses through all of me, and the intensity and recognition of it envelop my consciousness and I laugh with great joy. Something has changed, because the last time, they had to shield me from the random vibration of it. Now I can tolerate it easily...
>
> The tube seems to become larger as another joins it from one side, and another waveform melds into me and we become one. I recognise the other immediately, as it does me, and there is the great excitement of reunion, this other I and I. How could I have forgotten this! We move along together, happily exploring the adventures, experience and knowledge of the other. The tube widens again, and another I joins us, and the process repeats itself. Our waveforms are remarkably identical and our pattern grows stronger as they move in phase...
>
> The tube expands again and I am no longer concerned with its walls as still another I enters the waveform flow. This is particularly exciting, as it is the first I perceive as returning from a completely nonhuman sojourn. Yet the intermesh was near-perfect and we became so much more. Now we know that, somewhere, a consciously controlled physical tail, much like a monkey's, is useful in ways far more than balance and acting as a third hand for holding things. It can be a very efficient means of communication far beyond a super sign language and just as eloquent as the spoken word.
>
> Steadily and surely, one I after another joins us. With each, we become more aware and remember more of the total. How many does not seem important. Our knowledge and ability is so great that we do not bother to contemplate it. It is not

important. We are one.

At the end of this experience the voice of Monroe's collective echoes Phinn's higher self in describing the assistance that's always available to us while incarnate, although emphasising that it must be requested:

> We can and do monitor, supplement, and enhance the flow of the human learning experience, as well as other learning experiences of similar content throughout space-time. This we perform continuously at all levels of human awareness so as to prepare properly those entraining units of our prime energy for the entry and meld into the totality that we are becoming. It is the essence of our growth to do so. Such assistance and preparation is forthcoming from us only by request from one or more levels of consciousness within the entraining unit. Thereafter, a bonding is in effect through which many forms of communication pass between us until the ultimate transformation occurs.

To supplement all this, a fine set of detailed accounts of what it's like to encounter and merge with our supersoul are provided by William Buhlman:[7]

> As I stare the light becomes blinding. A part of me wants to turn away, but I don't. It feels as if the outer layers of myself are being burned away – my old concepts, beliefs, assumptions, and conclusions are incinerated by the intensity of the light. I can take no more and scream out, "What is this?" Instantly, I'm drawn within the light. My mind is overwhelmed as I realise that I have merged with a greater, more expansive part of myself. I suddenly understand that I am the engine of my life – I'm the creative force within me. I recognise that I have separated from myself. For several moments, the light and I are one. I feel a deep peace and interconnectedness I have never known before. For the first time I realise that I can create whatever reality I choose – my creative power is beyond my comprehension. I now know that I have limited myself by the ideas and beliefs I have accepted, and I recognise the need to

release all my limits, fears and expectations. A profound sense of empowerment sweeps through me as I scream inside, *I will remember this.*

I'm drawn to what appears to be a column of pure white light. As I move closer to the light, the sheer power of its radiation is overpowering. I stop and try to adjust... I slowly move forward and touch the light. An intense surge of energy flows through my entire being. I'm suddenly immersed in an ocean of pure knowledge. I'm flooded with memories of all I've been, all I've done, all that I am... I lie still and review the experience with a feeling of awe. I absolutely know that the column of white light was really me – not just another part of me, but the pure me, the very essence of all I am. Is it possible that we are really that incredible? Now I feel separated and alone; yet, at the same time, I feel connected to something far greater than I've ever imagined.

My awareness is blinded by the intensity of the light. I begin to back away and shield myself from the crushing energy. The entity continues to communicate with my mind. "I will adjust... Not many of your kind venture this far in... You are ready or you would not be here. All of us are where we should be. I was once as you and you shall be as I; we are all on a great journey together. Your perception of me is inaccurate. I am but a child compared to others who dwell within the universe. The possible evolution of consciousness is unlimited."

Of course these latter are further fine examples of just how dazzling encounters with our supersoul can be, and why initially they can be overwhelming and mistaken for contact with some sort of external divine being, even Source itself. More generally the combined accounts in this section make it clear just how much knowledge, wisdom and creative power is available to us if we would but acknowledge and access it. What is more it resides not within independent and external entities who are somehow much more advanced than us, but within our *own* supersoul consciousness – of which each of us is a holographic projection.

EQUALS NOT INFERIORS

Various of our sources follow this to its natural conclusion, insisting that we shouldn't regard ourselves as in any way inferior or subservient to our supersoul or to other aspects of it. From a channelled perspective, Seth for example suggests we should adopt a more collective view of our power as nascent gods: 'You are learning to be cocreators. You are learning to be gods as you now understand the term.' The Michael messages describe the purpose of evolution being for 'the created to evolve to become the creator'.[8] Neale Donald Walsch's source talks in exactly the same terms:[9] 'You are already a god. You simply do not know it.' Elsewhere they elaborate:[10]

> There is only one of you, but you are much larger than you think!.. You are a divine being, capable of more than one experience at the same 'time' – and able to divide your self into as many different 'selves' as you choose... You are a being of divine proportion, knowing no limitation. A part of you is choosing to know yourself as your presently-experienced identity. Yet this is by far not the limit of your being, although you think that it is.

If we now turn to our OOB pioneers, in case you need any further persuasion of just how divine and powerful you *already* are, here again is Leadbeater writing exactly a century ago:[11]

> Surely this view should be the greatest possible encouragement to the man working down here, this knowledge that he is a far grander and more glorious being in reality than he appears to be, and that there is a part of him – enormously the greater part – which has already achieved what he, as a personality, is trying to achieve; and that all that he has to do down here is to try to make himself a perfect channel for this higher and more real self; to do his work and to try to help others in order that he may be a factor, however microscopic, in forwarding the evolution of the world... The true man... is himself already divine; and all that he needs is to be able to realise himself in all the worlds and at all possible levels, so that

in them all the divine power through him may work equally, and so God shall be in all.

One emotive, first-hand report of the supersoul and its creative power comes from a source I haven't yet mentioned because it's slightly different – the wonderfully transcendental near-death experience of an American artist called Mellen-Thomas Benedict. He appeared to succumb to terminal cancer in 1982, but as he was being 'drawn towards the light' he asked to talk to it, to find out what it was and what was happening.[12] Immediately the light presented itself as various religious figures and other archetypes, before turning into 'a higher-self matrix' that represents 'a super-ancient part of ourselves':

> It became very clear to me that all the Higher Selves are connected as one being, all humans are connected as one being, we are actually the same being, different aspects of the same being... I saw this mandala of human souls. It was the most beautiful thing I have ever seen. I just went into it, and it was just overwhelming. It was like all the love you've ever wanted, and it was the kind of love that cures, heals, regenerates. As I asked the Light to keep explaining, I understood what the Higher Self matrix is. We have a grid around the planet where all the Higher Selves are connected. This is like a great company, a subtle level of energy around us, the spirit level, you might say.

Elsewhere he reflects on the nature of 'Godhood' and our powers of creation:

> I came back with the understanding that God is not there. God is here. That's what it is all about. So this constant search of the human race to go out and find God... God gave everything to us, everything is here – this is where it's at. And what we are into now is God's exploration of God through us. People are so busy trying to become God that they ought to realise that we are already God and God is becoming us. That's what it is really about... Individual identity is evolving like branches of a fractal; the group soul explores in our individuality... As I saw forever, I

came to a realm in which there is a point where we pass all knowledge and begin creating the next fractal, the next level. We have that power to create as we explore. And that is God expanding itself through us.

Meanwhile back in the earth plane, after his hospice worker found him clinically dead she continued to monitor him for a pulse and heartbeat for an hour-and-a-half, at which point he re-entered his body and fell out of bed trying to reach out for the light beyond the window. A scan three months later revealed his cancer had completely disappeared.

But perhaps the pièce de résistance is provided by Phinn. Here his 'higher self' is describing how its many different projections have contributed to the growth and evolution of the collective self, and paints a picture of the even more creative future that will soon open up for them all:

Each one has contributed immeasurably to my understanding of life on planet earth. Without them and those like them I would still be a monad, an indivisible unit of the divine, but I would be an empty one, an ocean of potential without any waves of activity. Now I am almost ready to help supervise the start-up and running of a new planetary being, if such a graduation should be my chosen mode of expression...

In such a situation I, and other monads, will be as shepherds rather than administrators, overseeing the development of sentience in a myriad of forms yet to be devised. Doubtless some of us will become revered as deities, and awarded attributes we have no desire to own, and others will be seen as angelic messengers, bringing divine instruction to a needy populace. These roles, though thrust upon us as incarnate beings project their desires upon our light, will be something we have to either adapt to or make allowance for. We will be immensely intelligent beings of light who will be called upon time and time again to manifest qualities and personas relevant to the emotional, mental and spiritual needs of the individuals and societies under our tutelage.

Our ability to access these roles has been completely

facilitated by the almost inestimable contribution of our many soul probes, as the data accumulated from their incarnate adventures provides us with an encyclopaedia of experiential reference points. So, again, let me emphasise that *we* are *you* as much as *you* are *us*. The monad and the soul are one. All that remains, all that ever remains, is for the incarnate personality to understand and embrace this.

MERGING WITH SUPERSOUL ONCE DISCARNATE

We are often warned of the many dangers that can be encountered in the afterlife planes. Usually these revolve around the Tibetan idea of 'hungry ghosts', or of hellish realms generally. Sadly I can confirm these are all too real.[13] Yet perhaps far more beguiling are the 'consensus realities' in the mid astral planes where probably far greater numbers of departed spirits remain trapped in illusory worlds of every conceivable type, thinking of them as their ultimate destination. It is fascinating to find that these include every variety of religious heaven ever constructed by human imagination and belief, but there are myriads more besides – and arguably this is the real meaning of 'addiction to the illusion' that I referred to briefly in the last chapter.[14]

A number of our channelled sources provide us with personal experience here. Philip Gilbert briefly reports that at one point he 'makes a big effort to merge, to blend all his aspects into one'.[15] Erik Medhus too briefly reports on how he can 'step into that energy where he has an awareness of all his lives'.[16] Meanwhile Frederic Myers puts it like this:[17] 'Here, in the after-death, we become more and more aware of this group soul as we make progress.' He goes on to describe what happens as our awareness expands:

> You will recognise how greatly power of will, mind and perception can be increased through your entry into the larger self. You continue to preserve your identity and your fundamental individuality. But you develop immensely in character and in spiritual force. You gather the wisdom of the

ages... through love which has a gravitational pull and draws you within the memories of those who are akin to your soul.

Frances Banks too describes her joy at reuniting with her 'group soul':[18]

My joy was deep and strong when I realised that I had, indeed, found my own group even though I knew myself to be only on the outer fringe of their activities... Now your light can mingle with their brilliance and become one in intensity. Thought and aspiration grow into joy and ecstasy... This is but the initial stage of a journey into light, during which the surviving entity is gradually reunited with the whole soul.

To sum up a hugely important section, the way we avoid becoming trapped in hellish or illusory realms after death is by always deliberately seeking to expand our awareness, wherever we find ourselves – so as to ultimately reconnect with our supersoul consciousness. We should never be content to stand still and stagnate. We have just seen how important it is for us to attempt to tap into our supersoul's knowledge and wisdom while incarnate, so how much more important is it that we attempt to do so in the afterlife?

Let us close this section with another wonderful quote from Buhlman:[19]

I am often asked what I will do when I take my final breath... I am not content to simply 'go to the light'. I am not content to accept past acquaintances and comfortable surroundings as my new reality. In fact, I am not content to settle for any form-based reality as my spiritual home. I absolutely know that there is so much more available beyond the realms of form. There exist magnificent dimensions of living light simply waiting for us; all we need do is awaken and accept their reality.

THE HOLOGRAPHIC SUPERSOUL

All this is exactly why I'd suggest that the concept of holographic soul consciousness remains equally if not more valid with the introduction of the supersoul, because these messages tell us that in a very real sense we *are* the entirety of our supersoul consciousness. To me this is far more immediate and real than being a full representation of something we can only vaguely define as 'Source'. What is more it seems that as supersouls we create whole new worlds and universes ourselves, so doesn't that make us quite divine enough without us having to look any further? Then there's the possibility raised by Tom Campbell in chapter 6 that the ultimate Source may have been a pretty primeval level of consciousness with very little awareness at all.

On that basis I propose that my original concept of the holographic soul requires only the simplest of reformatting, mainly by replacing the word *Source* with *our supersoul*:

> Soul consciousness is holographic. We are both individual aspects of our supersoul, and full holographic representations of it, all at the same time. However this does not mean that soul individuality is in itself an illusion. The principle of the hologram is that the part contains the whole, and yet is clearly distinguishable from it.

> The primary aim of all supersouls, in diversifying into all the many holographic soul aspects of themselves that operate in a multitude of realms throughout a multitude of universes, is to experience all that is and can be. So as individualised aspects of our supersoul we have been projected into this 'earth' reality to paint the best picture we can with the palette of 'birth givens' mixed for us by our supersoul.

To dovetail with this, I propose to formally define the supersoul as follows:

> A supersoul is a grouping of hundreds, maybe thousands, of souls. Myriads of supersouls are projecting soul aspects of themselves into this and myriad other realities, meaning they are very far from the ultimate consciousness. Yet to be fully connected to your supersoul is to have boundless

wisdom and creative power, and as a full holographic representation of it you are already more divine than you can hope to conceive – divine enough, even, to nullify further speculation about what lies beyond.

A NEW ERA OF SUPERCONSCIOUSNESS?

So finally we come to understand the full significance of the supersoul, and the reason I've coined such an emotive term. We *are* the 'creator gods' talked of in such reverent terms down through the ages, and our ability to create knows no bounds. In fact the only real constraints are the limitations of faith and belief that we ourselves choose to impose. We have boundless power and potential, and the free will to use that incredible capacity in whatever way we see fit. Perhaps it's finally time for us to wake up to the reality of who and what we really are, and I sincerely hope this volume and the other two in the series will go some way towards assisting that process.

It should be clear by now that I'm not claiming the concept of the supersoul is a new one. Actually I've been at pains to tie it into the theosophical concept of the monad, for example, and to what channelled sources and OOB pioneers have variously called the 'group soul', 'oversoul' or 'higher self'. I have merely coined a new term, precisely in the hope of avoiding the confusion surrounding the multiple meanings of the alternatives.

Nevertheless the hugely important messages about the supersoul contained within popular books by Monroe, Seth and Walsch, for example, have perhaps been somewhat overlooked or undervalued to date – lost in a sea of other fascinating information. That is why I've pulled them together, along with extracts from less well-known sources, in the hope that a compilation that concentrates exclusively on the concept may have more impact. Based on this material I've then developed a proper model of how different levels of soul consciousness operate – which I hope brings together a number of important ideas that might previously have been regarded as incompatible, to provide a coherent overall framework.

Maybe humanity is finally ready to step into the full power of its supersoul birthright, and to take on board a more sophisticated model of soul consciousness than the ones we've relied on for millennia. The sources who gifted us *The Spirits' Book* more than one hundred and fifty years ago made it clear that we're only given the information we're ready for at any particular point, and heralded the changes to come:[20]

> You do not teach children what you teach to adults, and you do not give to a new-born babe the food which he could not digest; there is a time for all things. Spirits have taught many things that men have not understood or have perverted, but that they are now capable of understanding aright. Through their teaching in the past, however incomplete, they have prepared the ground to receive the seed which is now about to fructify.

We are currently witnessing an ever-increasing and more objective exploration of other dimensions by those following in the footsteps of the OOB pioneers. More and more scientists are beginning to accept that consciousness isn't a fortuitous by-product of the material world, but its very progenitor. Taken together with many other developments that have been building for decades, are we finally poised on the brink of a major evolutionary breakthrough?

Are we ready to accept our true identity as *supersouls*? Now *there's* a future that would really take the game we call being human to the next level...

APPENDIX
Personal Applications of Supersoul Spirituality

I guess in some ways that by undertaking this exercise I could be likened to one of those 'mad scientists' who insist on experimenting on themselves to see if their theories work – except that rather than risking death I merely risk laying myself somewhat bare, and possibly making myself look a little foolish in some people's eyes. But if it provides others with useful insights into how to apply various aspects of our new model to their own lives, it will have been worth it.

LIFE PURPOSE AND GUIDANCE

Contrary to what I've believed for some time past, I no longer see my research and writing as an over-riding and relatively fixed life purpose that I chose in advance – or even one that was chosen for me. Consciousness in all its forms has a fundamental desire to expand and know itself better, and we as humans achieve this in all sorts of ways, from great scientists and philosophers to the apparently humblest mothers and fathers quietly and protectively raising their children. By a combination of birth-given traits and consciously taken decisions I happen to have tended towards spiritual philosophy.

I may have had a certain degree of predisposition towards this sort of contemplation, but if so it certainly didn't come out until relatively late in life. What is more, in as much as it seems I could just as easily have chosen *not* to take this path, or to have given it up when the going got tough, arguably it's my conscious choices far more than any subliminal life plan that have kept me on it. This would in turn mean that any insights or guidance I receive when

I'm writing are provided because my conscious actions and decisions to research spiritual models and so on *attract* them to me quite naturally, *not* because I'm being singled out for special help or knowledge.

BIRTH GIVENS AND INTERACTIONS WITH RESONANT SOULS

As an example of how different people vary in respect of their awareness of resonant souls, let me compare myself to a close friend who will remain nameless. She has only just started out on a spiritual path in an overt sense, but is extremely open and aware, and is making clear and vivid connections with various resonant souls in meditations. From these she's gaining huge insights that are helping her to understand and overcome her own challenges, and seem to be helping them too when they're open to it.

By contrast I'm relatively insensitive in that I don't make clear connections with my resonant souls even in meditation, although I've had some success under regression. People like me will typically have less information to work with unless we choose to enlist help, for example via regression therapy, which I did as a by-product of training as a therapist myself. But we'll see that actually a huge amount can be achieved *without* knowledge or awareness of our resonant souls, just by using our own ability for conscious analysis and decision making, and listening to intuitive promptings.

So here are some of the main challenges I've faced and how I'd now analyse them in the light of our new model.

VICTIMHOOD

In the opening chapter I briefly mentioned my own 'dark night of the soul' that occurred in 2011-12. During this time pretty much all aspects of my life fell apart and my sanity was genuinely tested at several points. No amount of regression therapy or meditation could find the root cause, and although I was aware I needed to try and stay as positive as possible because of the way we create our own reality, I was continually wondering whether it wasn't part of my 'life plan' to go to the extreme of suffering, perhaps so I could teach others something from my experience.

I can now see that was egotistical nonsense that prevented me from taking full responsibility for what I was creating. What is more every time I was hit by what seemed to be another 'kick in the teeth' I would revert to victim mode, sometimes for five minutes, sometimes for half an hour, occasionally curling up in bed and really wallowing in self-pity for several days. I wasn't behaving like this all the time by any means, and for much of it I was working hard on positivity and affirmations and trying to find ways of improving various aspects of my situation. But I also now realise that the occasional but intense negativity was enough to attract more challenges. Until one day when, finally, and in a moment of the deepest desperation, I was gifted some inner guidance on just how, when the going got tough, I was actually *preferring* victimhood to staying strong.

So where did this guidance come from? We have seen that it could have been my supersoul consciousness generally, or some wiser non-incarnate aspect of it, or a resonant soul who had already overcome this challenge. I don't know. What I do know, and all that really matters, is that I was open enough to it that, in that moment, I made a hugely committed *conscious* decision to *never* allow myself to play the victim again, come what may. What is more, although I was operating from a conventional reincarnation model at the time, I didn't try to work out what 'past' lives might have caused my experience and try to heal them at source. I just made a conscious decision in the now that victimhood was no longer going to be part of who I am.

That decision was fully tested only shortly afterwards when the partner with whom I'd been having a long-distance relationship for several years finally ended it by meeting someone else and falling even more in love with him than she'd been with me. It was hugely painful, yet I didn't allow myself to fall back into old habits, despite sore temptation. But did she and I have a soul contract whereby she would test me to my limits? At the time this may have been a comforting thought that lessened the pain, but I now rather doubt it. Under our new model I think it's pretty clear that I manifested a perfect victim's partner who was often emotionally and physically unavailable due to other complications in her own life, and who quite understandably became less attached to me as I went downhill. We don't need to resort to any other explanation.

More generally, was my dark night entirely self-created and unplanned? I would say *not* entirely, because I realised afterwards that a pattern of victimhood had been set up when, as a sensitive and shy child, I arrived at boarding school and was quite heavily bullied – until I found the strength to stick up for myself. This experience set up a victim archetype within me that was then easily reactivated all those years later. This would suggest a certain predisposition in my birth givens. But I could still have conquered my dark night far earlier if I'd been using our new model, had realised that nearly anything in our adult lives can be consciously redirected, and more than anything that *nowhere* in the spiritual rule-book – not that there is such a thing of course – does it say that growth and expansion can only be achieved by suffering.

REJECTION

On a related theme, it was only some time afterwards that I realised one of the very first 'past' lives I experienced during my regression training involved a boy whose brother married the love of both of their lives. It appeared that he let his sense of victimhood and rejection take over to such an extent that he spent forty years living alone, staring out at the nearby fields, before he finally died. My 'old-model' take on this was that when I was similarly rejected in favour of someone else in this life I conquered a challenge that had completely overwhelmed me in that other life, this time consciously choosing love rather than bitterness and self-pity.

But using our new model I can now see that that other personality is *not* me, but merely a resonant soul from my supersoul facing a similar challenge. I hope that what I've achieved may help him given that his life is simultaneous and still ongoing, and I'm sure it will if he's open to that guidance. But − and this is the key point − there was *no need at all* for me to have any awareness of him to take the conscious decisions I did about how I responded to the challenge of rejection in my own life.

ISOLATION

Another related theme is that of isolation. This has been particularly marked in the last few years when I've been living and working on my own, often with no partner to speak of, no children, and − during the dark night at least − precious few friends. I used to think this was perhaps my *major* life challenge, chosen in advance. But again I now realise that much of it has simply been the result of the conscious decisions I've made − for example to remain unmarried, or to pursue a career in writing, or to move around the country, and so on. So there may well have been no element of planning in this.

ANGER

Pretty much everyone shows *some* anger *sometimes*, and opinions vary about the extent to which this is healthy. All I can say is that nowadays I find my energy is generally such that, on the rare occasions I feel anger and express it, it feels horrible. Of course partners can bear the brunt of this emotion more than most, and a few years back I ran into difficulty in several relationships when I expressed quite strong anger without any great justification.

One of these occasions was during my regression therapy training, so on the next module I set the express intent to find the cause of these outbursts. I was relieved to find that they apparently came from a 'spirit attachment' who'd been rejected by his wife and had committed suicide, and who'd been with me since my childhood as part of a planned challenge for me. He was of course helped on his way. But even at the time I had my doubts; and now, if I was a betting man, I'd lay strong money on this having been a complete diversion on my part, to avoid responsibility.

APPENDIX

So where did the outbursts come from? I am not convinced this was any sort of predisposition that formed part of my birth givens, because I don't remember anger being a significant feature in my early life. Having said that I can't find much in the way of obvious reasons for it in my later life. One possibility *may* be that it's a trait I've started to manifest for one reason or another, that has then set up a new resonance with another soul with similar issues who might be 'stoking my fire' sometimes.

This is not dissimilar to the spirit attachment idea, and on the face of it would represent another abrogation of responsibility. Except that this time I'm not pretending the problem has magically gone away. Instead I'm accepting the unhelpful influence may still be there, and as a result I can set a deliberate intention to shut it out of my life – by making sure to keep an eye out for it, and to nip it in the bud if it surfaces. I am still taking responsibility and making a conscious and informed decision, but perhaps in this case it makes my dismissal of the emotion easier if I recognise that in large part it's originating outside of me – and I don't have to *own* it. What is more, again, I don't need to know any details about who this other soul might be, or the specific issues they're facing, to take this decision.

Having said that anger seems to be pretty rare in my life these days, so only time will tell if this approach works for me.

Let me sum up by attempting to extract some general guidelines out of this analysis, which may hopefully be applicable to us all. It would appear that if any challenge you're facing has roots that are easily traceable into your childhood, it's most likely to represent an element of your birth givens. If this isn't the case it's more likely to be something you've created, or attracted to you, by your actions and intentions along the way in this life. In either circumstance your challenge can be worsened by the influence of a resonant soul, but this is arguably more likely with a self-created challenge – especially if, for example, it's difficult to establish an obvious source for such a strong emotion in your *own* experience.

In either case, though, you don't need to have any detailed awareness of any other resonant souls to make conscious decisions about how to face the given challenge in your own life. This is because of the general rule that each of us is primarily responsible for creating our own experience. This means no other soul, no matter how resonant, can exert an unduly disruptive influence on us – unless we let them by continuing to believe in old models of past-life karma and so on – and nor, for that matter, can we on them. Having said that I can't discount the possibility that in rare cases this rule may be sufficiently broken, for whatever reason, that serious therapy of one sort or another might be required.

To close, this analysis confirms that we must take *responsibility* for everything in our life, even if it's just how we react to a challenge. It also shows that we should take full *credit* when we overcome a difficult challenge that might also help other resonant souls to move forwards. Above all, again, it shows that we have complete *freedom* to direct our life towards whatever purpose we choose, and the *power* to make that as ambitious as we like.

SOURCE REFERENCES

Publication details for the books referenced below can be found in the bibliography. All website references were accurate at the time of publication.

1 JOURNEY OF DISCOVERY

1. I discuss this in more detail in Appendix I. Meanwhile all this and much more is covered in my autobiographical *The God Who Sometimes Screwed Up*.

2 CONCEPTS OF GOD AND SOURCE

1. Bhagavad Gita 3:4–8; see Mascaro, *The Bhagavad Gita*, pp. 17–18.

2. Bhagavad Gita 5:20–3; see ibid., p. 29.

3. Taken from en.wikipedia.org/wiki/Buddhism#Rebirth.

4. See, for example, the current Dalai Lama's *The Heart of the Buddha's Path*, pp. 165, 184 and 191–2, although note that he tends to refer to *anatman*. For a summary of the different teachings and schools see p. 174, note 3.

5. Taken from a mixture of en.wikipedia.org/wiki/Anatta and en.wikipedia.org/wiki/Soul#Buddhism.

6. See, for example, www.lifewithoutacentre.com/essays-transcripts/what-is-nonduality.

7. Reading 2172:1; see Todeschi, *Edgar Cayce on the Akashic Records*, chapter 3, p. 47.

8. Austen, *The Teachings of Silver Birch*, pp. 60–1 and 174.

9. From Pathwork Lecture 152, 'Connection Between Ego and Universal Power', pp. 1 and 3. The 258 lectures can be downloaded individually for free from www.pathwork.org/lecturesObtainingUnedited.html. Alternatively for a summary see my paper *Introduction to Pathwork* at www.ianlawton.com/pathwork.html.

10. Aurobindo, *The Life Divine*, Book 2, chapter 3, pp. 387, 389, 391 and 403, and chapter 16, p. 689.

11. Lawton, *The Wisdom of the Soul*, under question 2.1.3.

12. The word *oversoul* seems to be primarily used in connection with the 'parable of the two birds' found for example in the Mundaka Upanishad [3.1.1]. Indeed when this is discussed on some websites the word *supersoul* is used, although I wasn't aware of this when that word first came to me. See for example:

- www.harekrsna.com/philosophy/truth/supersoul.htm

- www.krishna.com/topic-term/supersoul and

- www.yoga-philosophy.com/eng/2souldiff.htm.

However it's definitely *not* used in the main scholarly translations of these texts, and accordingly I felt I wouldn't be overstepping the mark if I appropriated it for the entirely different context in which I use it.

13. Blavatsky, *The Secret Doctrine*, Volume I, Proem, p. 17.

14. Fortune, *The Cosmic Doctrine*, chapter 12, p. 76 and chapter 18, p. 111.

15. Lawton, *Afterlife*, chapter 25, pp. 363–4.

3 CHANNELLED CLUES

1. Fortune, *The Cosmic Doctrine*, Introduction, pp. 1 and 10–13.

2. Ibid., Introduction II, pp. 14–18.

3. For the background see Stead, *After Death*, Preface, Introduction and Biography.

4. Ibid., Part 2, chapter 1, p. 54.

5. In fact the same is almost certainly true of many of us when we're asleep, even though we remain blissfully unaware of our nocturnal activities. See Lawton, *Afterlife*, chapter 19, p. 181.

6. Cummins, *The Road to Immortality*, chapter 6, pp. 29–30.

7. Ibid., chapter 9, p. 39.

8. Gilbert, *Philip in the Spheres*, Part 3, chapter 5, pp. 324–6.

9. For the background see Greaves, *Testimony of Light*, Biographical Introduction and Part 1, pp. 22–5.

10. Ibid., Part 1, pp. 116–17.

11. Roberts, *Seth Speaks*, Introduction, pp. xvi–xvii.

12. Roberts, *The Nature of Personal Reality*, Introduction, p. viii.

13. Roberts, *Seth Speaks*, chapter 7, p. 107.

14. Roberts, *The Unknown Reality Volume Two*, Appendix 18, p. 713.

15. Roberts, *Seth Speaks*, chapter 4, pp. 56–7 and chapter 22, pp. 403–4 and 406.

16. For the background see Swainson, *Gildas Communicates*, chapters 1 and 2.

17. Ibid., chapter 1, pp. 20–1.

18. Sandys, *The Awakening Letters*, p. 92.

19. For the background see the original Preface and updated Introduction to the modern edition of *Messages from Michael*.

20. Ibid., back cover.

21. This comes from the summary at www.michaelteachings.com.

22. Yarbro, *Messages from Michael*, chapter 1, pp. 19 and 21. Note that I have deliberately left out the middle part of the main quote that follows because it refers to conventional reincarnatory concepts that might be unhelpful to our understanding at this point.

23. Ibid., chapter 2, p. 34 and chapter 4, p. 59.

24. Walsch, *Conversations with God: Book One*, chapter 13, p. 197.

25. Walsch, *Conversations with God: Book Three*, chapter 12, p. 196.

4 OUT-OF-BODY ENCOUNTERS

1. This section is by necessity a brief introduction only. For a more advanced and in-depth discussion see Lawton, *Afterlife*, chapters 9 and 10.

2. This idea is found in the majority of modern OOB pioneers' books. See, for example, Vieira, *Projections of the Consciousness* (IAC, 2007), chapter 51, p. 186 and McKnight, *Cosmic Journeys*, chapter 20, p. 247. See also Lawton, *Afterlife*, chapter 26, pp. 370–4.

3. For example Buhlman includes a brief survey at the end of his first book, *Adventures Beyond the Body*. He then records the results of a broader survey with over 16,000 responses from 30 countries in his second, *Secrets of the Soul*; see Part 1 and Appendices 1 and 2.

4. Taken from Buhlman, *Secrets of the Soul*, chapter 7.

5. For example Monroe's team developed what they called Hemi-Sync, the method still used now; see www.monroeinstitute.org/resources/hemi-sync. The Lucid Light machine has been developed by two psychologists, Dirk Proeckl and Engelbert Winkler; see www.gesund-im-licht.at/en/die-hypnagoge-lichterfahrung/einfuehrung.html.

6. Myriad books are available on this topic. One excellent resource is the website of a leading British researcher, www.charliemorley.com.

7. For full bibliographies of OOB material see Peterson, *Out of Body Experiences*, pp. 267–78; and also obebibliography.info/general.htm.

8. For the background information on these two see, for example, their respective Wikipedia entries.

9. Leadbeater, *Clairvoyance*, chapter 2, pp. 42–3.

10. Ibid., chapter 9, pp. 152–3.

11. Ibid., chapter 4, pp. 62–3 and 70–1.

12. See, for example, www.blavatskyarchives.com/onthemonad.htm, which contains a variety of extracts from *The Secret Doctrine*.

13. Besant, *The Ancient Wisdom*, chapter 7, pp. 206–12.

14. Ibid, chapter 6, p. 192 and chapter 7, p. 202.

15. Leadbeater, *The Monad and Other Essays*, chapter 1, p. 20.

16. Ibid., chapter 1, p. 13.

17. Ibid., chapter 2, pp. 57–8.

18. Aurobindo, *The Integral Yoga*, chapter 7, pp. 199–200.

19. See en.wikipedia.org/wiki/Integral_psychology_(Sri_Aurobindo).

20. Aurobindo, *The Life Divine*, Book 1, chapter 28, p. 295.

21. Yram, *Practical Astral Projection*, Part 1, chapter 2, p. 23.

22. Ibid., Part 3, chapter 8.

23. Ibid., Part 2, chapter 1, p. 163.

24. Ibid., Foreword, p. 12.

25. Larsen, *My Travels in the Spirit World*, chapter 9, pp. 103–6.

26. Ophiel, *The Art and Practice of Astral Projection*, Section 1, p. 6, Section 2, p. 35 and Addenda, pp. 109–11.

27. Twitchell, *Eckankar*, chapter 7. He was also one of the few people to

affirm that early theosophists such as Leadbeater were engaged in OOB exploration.

28. See for example Black, *Ekstasy*, chapter 3.
29. For the background information see Twitchell, *Eckankar*, front page and Glossary, p. 230.
30. Ibid., chapter 5, pp. 85–94, chapter 6, p. 103, chapter 8, pp. 135–45, chapter 9, pp. 153–6 and chapter 11.
31. Ibid., chapter 2, p. 32, chapter 8, p. 147 and chapter 11, p. 204.
32. Taken from Atteshlis, *The Esoteric Teachings*, front cover flap and Glossary, p.191; and from www.researchersoftruth.org.
33. Ibid., chapter 1, p. 19.
34. Ibid., chapter 9, p. 104 and Glossary, p. 192.
35. Monroe, *Journeys Out of the Body*, chapter 19, p. 243.
36. Ibid., chapter 9, p. 135.
37. As described in Roberts, *The Nature of Personal Reality*, chapter 13, p. 207.
38. Monroe, *Far Journeys*, chapter 8, pp. 94–8.
39. Ibid., chapter 9, p. 122.
40. Monroe's third book, *Ultimate Journey*, was published in 1993 just a year before he died. In this he adds some new concepts, in particular coining the term EXCOM, or the 'Executive Committee' of his 'I-There' that 'emerged from the many life personalities each of us contain' (Glossary, pp. 272–3). There is some reasonable confusion about exactly what he meant by terms such as INSPEC and EXCOM, because he never really related them to existing concepts so that we might get a proper handle. To make matters worse he seems to contradict himself in places. For example, in this third book he refers to his I-There as having been the unseen navigator in most of his OOBEs (chapter 11, p. 142), but this is exactly how he refers to his INSPECs in *Far Journeys* (chapter 8, pp. 91–4). What is more in *Journeys Out of the Body* he uses the term I-There to describe what he took to be another version of himself living in a different although earth-like world that he refers to as Locale III (chapter 6, p. 96). Nevertheless overall I think it's fair to propose that his concept of INSPECs bears close comparison with that of the supersoul.

41. McKnight, *Cosmic Journeys,* chapter 14, p. 160 and chapter 20, pp. 242–4.

42. McKnight, *Soul Journeys,* chapter 1, pp. 10–14.

43. See Moen, *Voyages into the Unknown*, chapter 3, pp. 56–60 and www.afterlife-knowledge.com/disk.html. Note that, as with Michael at the end of the last chapter, I've deliberately left out the middle part of the main quote that follows because it refers to conventional reincarnatory concepts that might be unhelpful to our understanding at this point. Note also that Moen spends most of the rest of this first book and much of the next two describing his retrieval work with trapped consciousnesses, which he learned during various 'Lifeline Program' courses at the Monroe Institute. Many of these missions took the form of 'partnered explorations' in which he would meet up with other Institute graduates while OOB, they would do the work together and then compare notes when back in the physical. For all that these notes showed the sort of superficial differences we might expect owing to subjective interpretation of other-plane events, the impressive underlying correlations were themselves highly evidential of a whole string of at least partly objective experiences. It is also interesting to note that his main guide, who he referred to as 'coach' and who often accompanied him on these missions, is unequivocally described as another aspect of his disk, and acts as the main channel for communication with all the other aspects (chapter 6, pp. 171 and 204–5).

44. Moen, *Voyage to Curiosity's Father*, chapter 22, p. 199 and chapter 28, p. 237.

45. In 2013 Buhlman did produce a third, *Adventures in the Afterlife*, but this is a largely fictional account – albeit loosely based on his own experiences.

46. Buhlman, *The Secret of the Soul*, chapter 1, pp. 14–15 and 20, chapter 2, p. 42 and chapter 4, pp. 65 and 74.

47. Personal correspondence, 8 December 2012.

48. Bruce, *Astral Dynamics*, chapter 7, p. 59.

49. Taylor, *Soul Traveller*, chapter 9, pp. 99–100.

50. Phinn, *More Adventures in Eternity*, p. 114. In fact his guides later reveal that these are merely more lucid recollections of his work the

night before that he didn't remember.

51. Ibid., Introduction, p. 5.

52. Ibid., p. 199.

53. Ibid., p. 270.

54. This actually comes from a first draft of the manuscript before it was published.

55. Ziewe, *Multidimensional Man*, p. 191.

56. Extracted from Ziewe's paper *The Super Dimensions Part 1* at www.multidimensionalman.com; the reference to this being his 'higher aspect or soul' comes from personal correspondence dated 8 April 2013.

57. All the following comes from Aardema, *Explorations in Consciousness*, chapter 6, pp. 176–7, 183 and 188.

5 TIME, CONCURRENT LIVES AND THE LAW OF ATTRACTION

1. Stobaeus Excerpt 16; see Scott, *Hermetica*, p. 173.

2. Timaeus 7; see Lee, *Plato: Timaeus and Critias*, p. 52.

3. See Swainson, *Gildas Communicates*, chapter 8, p. 109, and Walsch, *Conversations with God: Book Two*, chapter 3, p. 28.

4. These quotes are taken from Lawton, *The Power of You*, chapter 2, pp. 37–8. They come from Abraham (see Hicks, *The Law of Attraction*, Part 4); from Jeshua (see *The Way of Mastery*, Volume 1, Lesson 3); from the Pathwork Guide (see Lecture 112, dated 01 March 1963 at www.pathwork.org/the-lectures); and from Ramtha (see Knight, *The White Book*, chapter 13).

5. This background information is broadly a summary of Capra, *The Tao of Physics*, chapter 4, pp. 71–4 and chapter 12, pp. 177–207.

6. Atteshlis, *The Esoteric Teachings*, chapter 8, p. 92.

7. Sherwood, *Post-Mortem Journal*, chapter 7, p. 29. For other quotes from departed spirits about time and space in the astral see Lawton, *Afterlife*, chapter 23, pp. 282–7.

8. Sherwood, *The Country Beyond*, chapter 4, p. 71 and chapter 6, pp. 94–5.

9. Monroe, *Journeys Out of the Body*, chapter 5, p. 74.

10. Richelieu, *A Soul's Journey*, chapter 11, p. 186.

11. Greaves, *Testimony of Light*, Part 1, p. 84.

12. Medhus, *My Life After Death*, chapter 15, p. 109.

13. Leadbeater, *The Monad and Other Essays*, chapter 5, pp. 85–7; the Blavatsky quote is reported to come from *The Secret Doctrine*, Volume I, p. 69.

14. Walsch, *Conversations with God: Book Two*, chapter 3, pp. 28–9.

15. Ibid., chapter 19, p. 235.

16. Walsch, *Conversations with God: Book Three*, chapter 6, p. 108.

17. Roberts, *Seth Speaks*, chapter 4, pp. 56 and 60, chapter 22 and Appendix.

18. Walsch, *Conversations with God: Book Three*, chapter 2, p. 52 and *Book Two*, chapter 5, p. 67.

19. See www.eliasforum.org/transcripts.html, transmission dated 28 June 1997.

20. Medhus, *My Life After Death*, chapter 21, p. 133.

21. Ziewe, *Multidimensional Man*, Part 1, p. 55.

22. McKnight, *Cosmic Journeys*, chapter 15, p. 168.

23. Lawton, *Afterlife*, chapter 25, pp. 362–9.

6 A DIGITAL UNIVERSE?

1. None of the many reports of 'out-of-place artifacts' or OOPARTS that have been touted by alternative historians for decades stand up to close scrutiny; see my paper *Anomalous Artifacts* at www.ianlawton.com/gu8.html. Similarly the best known source of reports of extremely ancient modern human remains is Michael Cremo and Richard Thompson's *Forbidden Archaeology* (Bhaktivedanta Institute, 1993). However they're even more selective in their use of evidence than the orthodox scholars they attempt to critique; see my paper *Problems With Anomalous Human Remains* at www.ianlawton.com/gu2.html

2. For the background information see Campbell, *My Big T.O.E.*, Book 1, Section 1; and in particular chapter 9, p. 79 (binaural beats) and chapters 13–14 (early OOBEs).

3. What follows summarises ibid., Book 1, Section 2, chapters 24–34.

4. For a more detailed discussion of this see Lawton, *Afterlife*, chapter 1.

5. For a more detailed discussion of this see Lawton, *Atlantis: The Truth*, chapter 8, p. 109 – albeit that this idea is in part based on a mistranslation of the Greek word for chaos that actually means 'chasm' or 'void'.

6. This paragraph and what follows in the next section is a summary of Campbell, *My Big T.O.E.*, Book 3, Section 5, chapters 76–83. For a graphic representation of the systems and subsystems see chapter 76, p. 654.

7. Ibid., Book 3, Section 5, chapter 82, p. 701.

8. Walsch, *Conversations with God: Book Three*, chapter 6, p. 118.

9. Campbell, *My Big T.O.E.*, Book 1, Section 1, chapter 10, pp. 87–8.

10. See, for example, *The Wisdom of the Soul*, chapter 4, pp. 121–3.

11. I have argued against this idea at length and, as far as I can tell, in his whole three volumes of genuinely science-based spirituality Campbell doesn't refer to it once; (see, for example, *The Big Book of the Soul*, chapter 8, pp. 238–41).

12. Extracted from Ziewe's paper *The Super Dimensions Part 4* at www.multidimensionalman.com.

13. Dack, *The Out-of-the-Body Experience*, chapter 13, pp. 293–5.

14. Monroe, *Journeys Out of the Body*, chapter 6, pp. 94–100.

15. For a more detailed discussion of these and other cases, and their possible interpretations, see Lawton, *Afterlife*, chapter 7, pp. 60–3.

16. See, for example, ibid., chapter 21, pp. 231–40.

17. Campbell, *My Big T.O.E.*, Book 3, Section 5, chapter 78, p. 667.

7 SUPERSOUL SPIRITUALITY

1. Lawton, *Afterlife*, chapter 22, pp. 263–79.

2. The evidence from all the pioneers is compared and analysed in Lawton, *The Big Book of the Soul*, chapters 5 and 6. The supporting channelled and other material relating to the interlife is in chapter 7, pp. 210–31.

3. Lawton, *Afterlife*, chapter 27, pp. 401–3.
4. Leadbeater, *The Monad and Other Essays*, chapter 5, p. 86.
5. See www.eliasforum.org/transcripts.html, transmission dated 5 November 1999.
6. Roberts, *The Nature of Personal Reality*, chapters 15 and 19.
7. Walsch, *Conversations with God: Book Three*, chapter 14.
8. Walsch, *Conversations with God: Book Two*, chapter 5, pp. 66–7.
9. Aardema, *Explorations in Consciousness*, chapter 6, p. 188; he actually references Monroe's *Ultimate Journey* at this point but with no specific details.
10. Ziewe, *Multidimensional Man*, p. 191.
11. Phinn, *More Adventures in Eternity*, pp. 121, 125 and 129.
12. Again this comes from a first draft of the manuscript of *You Are History* before it was published.
13. Taken from www.afterlife-knowledge.com/disk.html.
14. Medhus, *My Life After Death*, chapter 9, p. 74.
15. Taken from www.afterlife-knowledge.com/disk.html.
16. The main parts that cover the most relevant material are DeMarco, *The Cosmic Internet*, chapter 2, pp. 38–43 and 54–9, and chapter 3, pp. 99–102 and 107–13.
17. Cummins, *The Road to Immortality*, chapter 6, p. 30.
18. Taken from a mixture of en.wikipedia.org/wiki/Rebirth_(Buddhism) and en.wikipedia.org/wiki/Skandha.

8 WE ARE THE GODS!
1. Assante, *The Last Frontier*, Introduction, pp. 17–18.
2. Roberts, *Seth Speaks*, chapter 4, pp. 58–9 and 61.
3. Leadbeater, *The Monad*, chapter 2, p. 55.
4. Yram, *Practical Astral Projection*, Part 1, chapter 11, pp. 84–5.
5. Phinn, *More Adventures in Eternity*, p. 174.
6. Monroe, *Far Journeys*, chapter 9, pp. 120–2.
7. Buhlman, *Adventures Beyond the Body*, chapter 2, pp. 47, 55–7 and 60–1.

SOURCE REFERENCES

8. Yarbro, *Messages from Michael*, chapter 1, p. 23.

9. Walsch, *Conversations with God: Book One*, chapter 13, p. 202.

10. Walsch, *Conversations with God: Book Two*, chapter 5, pp. 64–5.

11. Leadbeater, *The Monad and Other Essays*, chapter 1, pp. 24–5.

12. From www.near-death.com/experiences/reincarnation04.html.

13. They are described in great detail in Lawton, *Afterlife*, chapters 14–18.

14. For a more detailed discussion of this see ibid., chapter 25.

15. Gilbert, *Philip in the Spheres*, Part 3, chapter 3, p. 291.

16. Medhus, *My Life After Death*, chapter 21, p. 133.

17. Cummins, *The Road to Immortality*, chapter 6, p. 30 and *Beyond Human Personality*, chapter 4, p. 42.

18. Greaves, *Testimony of Light*, Part 2, pp. 137–8 and Part 1, p. 119.

19. Buhlman, *The Secret of the Soul*, chapter 8, p. 144.

20. Kardec, *The Spirits' Book*, Book 3, chapter 8, p. 326 and Book 4, chapter 2, p. 407.

BIBLIOGRAPHY

This bibliography is limited to the books specifically referenced in this work. The details given below are for the imprint or edition consulted, although the original date of publication quoted in the main text may have been earlier.

OUT-OF-BODY EXPERIENCES

Aardema, Frederick, *Explorations in Consciousness*, Mount Royal Publishing, 2012.

Atteshlis, Stylianos, *The Esoteric Teachings*, The Stoa Series, 1992.

Besant, Annie, *Ancient Wisdom: An Outline of theosophical Teachings*, Kessinger Publishing, 1998 (first published 1898).

Black, David, *Ekstasy*, Bobbs-Merrill, 1975.

Bruce, Robert, *Astral Dynamics*, Hampton Roads, 2009.

Buhlman, William, *Adventures Beyond the Body*, HarperOne, 1996.

Buhlman, William, *The Secret of the Soul*, HarperOne, 2001.

Buhlman, William, *Adventures in the Afterlife*, CreateSpace, 2013.

Campbell, Thomas, *My Big T.O.E.* (3 volumes in one), Lightning Strike Books, 2007.

Crookall, Robert, *The Study and Practice of Astral Projection*, Citadel Press, 1976 (first published 1960).

Dack, Graham, *The Out-of-Body Experience*, OOBEX Publishing, 1999.

Fox, Oliver (Hugh Callaway), *Astral Projection*, Citadel Press, 1962 (first published 1938).

Green, Celia, *Out-of-the-Body Experiences*, Institute of Psychophysical Research, 1968.

Larsen, Caroline, *My Travels in the Spirit World*, Tuttle, 1927.

Leadbeater, Charles Webster, *Clairvoyance*, Theosophical

BIBLIOGRAPHY

Publishing Society, 1899.

Leadbeater, Charles Webster, *The Monad and Other Essays*, Theosophical Publishing House, 1929 (first published 1920).

McKnight, Rosalind, *Cosmic Journeys: My Out-of-Body Explorations with Robert A Monroe*, Hampton Roads, 1999.

McKnight, Rosalind, *Soul Journeys: My Guided Tours Through the Afterlife*, Hampton Roads, 2005.

Moen, Bruce, *Voyage into the Unknown*, Hampton Roads, 1997.

Moen, Bruce, *Voyage Beyond Doubt*, Hampton Roads, 1998.

Moen, Bruce, *Voyages into the Afterlife*, Hampton Roads, 1999.

Moen, Bruce, *Voyage to Curiosity's Father*, Hampton Roads, 2001

Monroe, Robert, *Journeys Out of the Body*, Broadway Books, 2001 (first published 1971).

Monroe, Robert, *Far Journeys*, Doubleday, 1985.

Monroe, Robert, *Ultimate Journey*, Broadway Books, 2000.

Muldoon, Sylvan and Carrington, Hereward, *Projection of the Astral Body*, Rider, 1929.

'Ophiel' (Edward Peach), *The Art and Practice of Astral Projection*, Weiser Books, 1974 (first published 1961).

Peterson, Robert, *Out of Body Experiences*, Hampton Roads, 1997.

Phinn, Gordon, *Eternal Life and How to Enjoy It*, Hampton Roads, 2004.

Phinn, Gordon, *More Adventures in Eternity*, O Books, 2008.

Phinn, Gordon, *You Are History*, White Crow Books, 2015.

Richelieu, Peter, *A Soul's Journey*, Thorsons, 1996 (first published 1953).

Taylor, Albert, *Soul Traveller: A Guide to Out-of-Body Experiences and the Wonders Beyond*, New American Library, 2000.

Turvey, Vincent, *The Beginnings of Seership: Astral Projection, Clairvoyance and Prophecy*, University Books, 1969 (first published 1909).

Twitchell, Paul, *Eckankar: The Key to Secret Worlds*, Illuminated Way Publishing, 1987.

'Yram' (Marcel Forhan), *Practical Astral Projection*, Samuel Weiser, 1974 (first published under the title *Le Médecin de l'Âme* in 1925).

Ziewe, Jurgen, *Multidimensional Man*, Lulu.com, 2008.

CHANNELLED, OCCULT AND ESOTERIC

Assante, Julia, *The Last Frontier: Exploring the Afterlife and Transforming Our Fear of Death*, New World Library, 2012.

Aurobindo, Sri, *The Life Divine*, Lotus Press, 1990 (first published 1939 and earlier).

Aurobindo, Sri, *The Integral Yoga*, Lotus Press, 1993.

Blavatsky, Helena, *The Secret Doctrine* (2 volumes), Theosophical University Press, 1988 (first published 1888).

Capra, Fritjof, *The Tao of Physics*, Flamingo, 1992 (first published 1975).

Cummins, Geraldine, *The Road to Immortality*, White Crow Books, 2012 (first published 1932).

Cummins, Geraldine, *Beyond Human Personality*, White Crow Books, 2013 (first published 1935).

Dalai Lama, His Holiness the, *The Heart of the Buddha's Path*, HarperCollins, 2011.

DeMarco, Frank, *The Cosmic Internet*, Rainbow Ridge Books, 2011.

Fortune, Dion, *The Cosmic Doctrine*, Samuel Weiser, 2000 (first published 1949).

Gilbert, Alice, *Philip in the Spheres*, The Aquarian Press, 1952.

Greaves, Helen, *Testimony of Light*, Rider, 2005 (first published 1969).

Hicks, Esther and Jerry, *The Law of Attraction*, Hay House, 2007.

Jeshua via Jayem, *The Way of Mastery* (3 volumes), Heartfelt Publishing PMA, 1995.

Kardec, Allan, *The Spirits' Book*, Cosimo Classics, 2006 (first published 1857).

Knight, JZ, *Ramtha: The White Book*, JZK Publishing, 2004.

Lee, Desmond, *Plato: Timaeus and Critias*, Penguin Classics, 1977.

Mascaro, Juan (trans.), *The Bhagavad Gita*, Penguin Classics, 2003.

Medhus, Erik and Elisa, *My Life After Death*, Atria Books, 2015.

Roberts, Jane, *Seth Speaks*, Bantam, 1974.

Roberts, Jane, *The Unknown Reality: Volume Two*, Prentice Hall,1979.

Roberts, Jane, *The Nature of Personal Reality*, Bantam, 1978.

Sandys, Cynthia, *The Awakening Letters*, Neville Spearman, 1978.

Sandys, Cynthia, *The Awakening Letters: Volume Two*, CW Daniel, 1986.

Scott, Walter, *Hermetica*, Solos Press, 1992.

Sherwood, Jane, *The Country Beyond*, CW Daniel, 1991 (first published in 1944).

Sherwood, Jane, *Post-Mortem Journal: Communications from TE Lawrence*, Divine Truth, 1964.

Stead, William, *After Death: Letters from Julia*, CreateSpace, 2012 (first published 1905).

Swainson, Mary and White, Ruth, *Gildas Communicates*, Neville Spearman, 1971.

The Way of Mastery (3 volumes), Shanti Christo Foundation, 2009.

Todeschi, Kevin, *Edgar Cayce on The Akashic Records*, ARE Press, 1998.

Walsch, Neale Donald, *Conversations with God* (3 volumes), Hodder & Stoughton, 1997-9.

Yarbro, Chelsea Quinn, *Messages from Michael*, Caelum Press, 2005 (first published 1979).

INDEX

INDEX

47–8, 52–3, 71, 110, 121, 125
Lehmann, Rosamond, 37
McKnight, Rosalind, 56–7, 78
Mennerich, Dennis, 84, 90
Moen, Bruce, 1, 57, 60, 116–18
Monroe, Robert, 4, 12, 43, 54–8, 69, 80, 84, 90, 92, 122–3, 131
Muhammad, 41
Muldoon, Sylvan, 49
Myers, Frederic, 30, 32, 118, 128
Nanak, Guru, 52
Newton, Michael, 9, 11, 104
Ophiel (aka Edward Peach), 52
Phinn, Gordon, 1, 60, 113, 116, 121, 123, 127
Pierrakos, Eva, 21
Plato, 64
Pythagoras, 52
Ramster, Peter, 10
Redfield, James, 7
Regardie, Israel, 52
Roberts, Jane, 33–4, 36, 55, 90
Rumi, Jalaluddin, 52

Sandys, Cynthia, 37
Sitchin, Zecharia, 94
Socrates, 52
St John, 41
St Paul, 41
Stead, William, 29, 122
Stevenson, Ian, 9
Swainson, Mary, 36
Swedenborg, Emanuel, 41
Tabrizi, Shamus, 52
Talbot, Michael, 22
Taylor, Albert, 59
Tomlinson, Andy, 10
Tulsidas, Goswami, 52
Turvey, Vincent, 49
Twitchell, Paul, 52
Walsch, Neale Donald, 39, 64, 70, 72, 74, 77, 90, 112, 125, 131
White, Ruth, 36
Yarbro, Chelsea Quinn, 37–8
Yogananda, Paramhansa, 41
Yram (aka Marcel Forhan), 49–50, 121
Yukteswar, Sri, 41
Ziewe, Jurgen, 1, 61, 78, 91, 113
Zoroaster, 41

THE SUPERSOUL SERIES

all published by Rational Spirituality Press *www.rspress.org*
see also *www.ianlawton.com*

RESEARCH BOOKS

[Volume 1] SUPERSOUL (2013) is the main reference book for Supersoul Spirituality, containing out-of-body and channelled evidence that each and every one of us is a holographic reflection of a supersoul that has power way beyond our wildest imaginings.

[Volume 2] THE POWER OF YOU (2014) compares modern channelled wisdom from a variety of well-known sources, all emphasising that each of us is consciously or unconsciously creating every aspect of our own reality, and that this is what the current consciousness shift is all about.

[Volume 3] AFTERLIFE (2019) is a state-of-the-art, clear, reliable guide to the afterlife based on the underlying consistencies in traditional channelled material and modern out-of-body research.

SIMPLE BOOKS

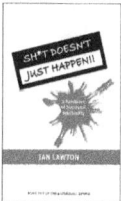

SH*T DOESN'T JUST HAPPEN!! (2016) introduces Supersoul Spirituality by explaining how and why we ourselves create or attract everything we experience in our adult lives... so that we are never victims of chance, God's will, our karma or our life plans.

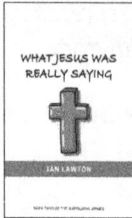

WHAT JESUS WAS REALLY SAYING (2016) is a fundamental reinterpretation of the Christian message that uses excerpts from the Gospels to propose that, through his supposed miracles, Jesus was trying to show us that each of us is a creator god of the highest order and can manipulate the illusion we call reality at will.

THE GOD WHO SOMETIMES SCREWED UP (2018) charts the author's progression from motorcycle and car racer, to pyramid explorer and researcher of ancient civilisations, to spiritual philosopher... with analysis and examples of how he has created or manifested all the various aspects of his life, both good and bad.

DEATH IS AN ADVENTURE!! (2019) is a simple yet essential guide to the afterlife, which answers all your questions such as why you will continue to exist, what to expect and how best to prepare. Based on evidence not belief, it describes the unlimited possibilities we have to create wondrous new experiences... as long as we have a reliable map of the territory.

THE PREHISTORIC TRUTH SERIES

all published by Rational Spirituality Press *www.rspress.org*
see also *www.ianlawton.com*

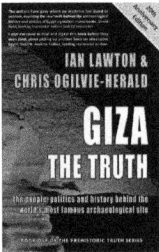

[Volume 1] GIZA: THE TRUTH (2020) is the 20th anniversary edition of this celebrated book, which thoroughly investigates how, why and when the most famous archaeological monuments in the world were built... in the process placing grave doubt on the multitude of alternative theories that surround them.

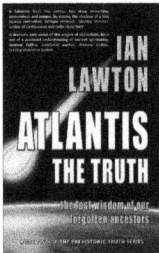

[Volume 2] ATLANTIS: THE TRUTH (2020) is a reinterpretation of the most revered ancient texts and traditions from all around the world that postulates a forgotten, highly cultured but not technologically advanced 'golden race' who were wiped out in a global catastrophe around 13,000 years ago... with supporting geological and other evidence suggesting where, when and how this 'Atlantean' race most likely lived.

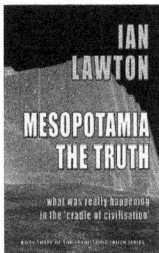

[Volume 3] MESOPOTAMIA: THE TRUTH (2020) is an investigation into what was really going on in what is perhaps the definitive cradle of civilisation, and what elements of modern living were introduced for the first time... coupled with a thorough rebuttal of alternative interpretations of its texts concerning supposed extraterrestrial visitors who genetically created humankind.

IAN LAWTON was born in 1959. Formerly an accountant, sales exec, business and IT consultant and avid bike and car racer, in his mid-thirties he changed tack completely to become a writer-researcher specialising in ancient history and, more recently, spiritual philosophy. His first two books, *Giza: The Truth* and *Genesis Unveiled*, sold over 30,000 copies worldwide.

In his *Books of the Soul Series* he originated the ideas of Rational Spirituality and of the holographic soul. But since 2013 he has been developing the more radical worldview of Supersoul Spirituality in the *Supersoul Series*. (A short film clip discussing the latter can be found at *www.ianlawton.com* and on YouTube.) In 2020 he updated and republished his earlier works on ancient history as the *Prehistoric Truth Series*.

www.ingramcontent.com/pod-product-compliance
Lightning Source LLC
Chambersburg PA
CBHW051425090426
42737CB00014B/2829

* 9 7 8 0 9 5 7 2 5 7 3 3 7 *